# WHAT OTHERS SAY ABOUT THIS BOOK

*As a mother whose daughter was murdered, as a psychiatrist and as a member of the Board of Parents of Murdered Children, I want to thank you from the bottom of my heart. I will certainly be recommending your book to others.*

Dr. Wanda L. Bincer, M.D., Madison, Wisconsin

*You've managed to put together a knowledgeable, compassionate, and factual book to help those of us who have been suddenly thrust into the unwilling role of victims. God bless you for your insight and wisdom, and I thank you from the bottom of my heart for your lifeline.*

Patricia O'Connor - Mother of Victim, Jackson, New Jersey

*This book is invaluable for Hospice Counselors, and for families grieving a violent death. It adds priceless emotional and practical information about loss and grief.* No Time For Goodbyes *is rich with personal testament to the love and courage of survivors.*

Joyce Dace-Lombard, MFCC, Bereavement Coordinator and Counselor, Camarillo Hospice, Camarillo, CA

No Time For Goodbyes *will become one of the most publicized books I can verbalize to any surviving family member I come in contact with. I never thought I could curl up with a good book, and spend most of the time 'crying.'*

Donna E. Lamonaco, Surviving spouse of victim, Concerns of Police Survivors (COPS) - Brandywine, Maryland

*There is sound advice here, not only for those who are grieving a violent death, but for those who want to comfort them.*

"Sydney Morning Herald" Review, Sydney, Australia

No Time For Goodbyes *is designed for anyone who wants the self-affirming skills of full emotional expression for victim survivors and to understand the options generated can be empowering. This is the most significant book that I have read on this tragic subject.*

Dr. Earl A. Grollman, Author of *Living When A Loved One Has Died,* Belmont, MA.

*I wanted to thank you for putting into words the heartbreak and utter devastation one feels when a loved one has been suddenly taken from you in death.*

Mrs. Gloria Cook, Mother of murdered son - Gibsonia, PA

*Ms. Lord provides excellent practical susggestions for coming to grips with grief, and for coping with specific problems encountered.*

Traumagram, Literature Review, Newsletter, American Trauma Society

*As part of our counseling, we have discovered that the use of* No Time For Goodbyes *is helpful in giving families tools to reach some resolution of their loss.*

Judy Batchelor, Project Director, The Family Bereavement Center, Detroit, MI.

*For fifteen months your book stayed in my purse and with me twenty-four hours a day. I now keep it along side my bed. Thanks so very much, Janice. Though I've never met you, you are the one that gave me the strength to keep going.*

Cindi Kay Winkle, Survivor of murdered fiance - Aumsville, Oregon

*Why didn't I find your book two years ago. It seems like an eternity since I journeyed to that black pit of emotions within. Your words helped me realize how far I've come and at times when I feel the shadow of that time, I can pick it up and realize I'm not alone.*

Sue Look, Survivor of a murdered friend, South Perth, Australia

*An excellent book of compassionate and practical advice for those grieving for a loved one killed by violence or accident. A particularly good chapter is "Coping With The Criminal Justice System."*

Nolo Press, California

*This book should be in the hands of every victim of a homicide. To my knowledge there is no other resource that touches this unique group of people.*

Rhonda Anthony, MADD - Fresno, CA.

*I couldn't make sense out of this world any longer after the murders of my sister and my niece. Your book has helped me a great deal. Thank you for writing such a helpful book.*

Sandra Mulcah, Survivor, St. Paul, Minn.

# NO TIME FOR GOODBYES

## Coping with Sorrow, Anger, and Injustice

### After A Tragic Death

# NO TIME FOR GOODBYES

Coping with Sorrow, Anger, and Injustice

After A Tragic Death

By

Janice Harris Lord

Pathfinder Publishing of California
Ventura, CA

# NO TIME FOR GOODBYES

Published By:
Pathfinder Publishing
458 Dorothy Avenue
Ventura, CA 93003, U.S.A.

First Printing 1987
Second Edition January 1988 Revised
Third Printing 1989
Third Edition 1990 Revised
Fifth Printing 1990
Fourth Edition 1991 Revised
Seventh Printing 1992
Eighth Printing 1993
Ninth Printing 1994
Tenth Printing 1995
Eleventh Printing 1996
Twelfth Printing 1997

Library of Congress Cataloging-in-Publication Data

Lord, Janice Harris.
    No time for goodbyes : coping with sorrow, anger, and injustice after a tragic death / by Janice Harris Lord. — 4th ed., rev.
        p. cm.
    Includes bibliographical references and index.
    ISBN 0-934793-40-9 : $11.95
    1. Bereavement — Psychological aspects. 2. Violent deaths — Psychological aspects. 3. Grief. I. Title.
BF575.G7L66   1991
155.9'37 — dc20                                   91-31702
                                                  CIP

ISBN 0-934793-40-9

# DEDICATION

To the countless victims of violence who dared to open their hearts to me and thereby carved into my heart a deepened capacity to care. I can never fully understand your pain, but I treasure your willingness to allow me to stand with you in your suffering.

# ACKNOWLEDGEMENTS

Many people planted seeds throughout the years which have now blossomed into this book. So many colleagues have contributed to its evolution that it is difficult to number them. And it is the victims themselves who breathe life into its pages. I can never name all of them.

A major note of gratitude goes to Dr. Dennis Saleeby, my graduate social work professor, who required readings about death and dying before it was popular. It was in his class that I developed my first workshop on the subject. That was a major seed.

I am deeply indebted to Dr. Robert Weiss of the Work and Family Research Unit at University of Massachusetts for believing that my papers and brochures for families in which a loved one has been killed were valuable. Through his inspired paper, *Will It Always Feel This Way?—For the Parent Whose Child Has Been Killed,* he confirmed for me that it is respectable to write from the heart. He has been an inspiration whose influence will continue beyond his years.

I am grateful to Dr. Hannelore Wass, Dr. Camille Wortman, Darrin Lehman, and Dr. Therese Rando for their excellent research and publications which have formed an invaluable cornerstone for my work with victims. I especially thank them for reviewing the book during their busy schedules.

Thanks go to Joyce Dace Lombard, Dr. Judy Alexandre, Ron Hillestad and Dr. Kathleen Wheeler for their helpful text suggestions.

I thank Judge Cathy Stayman Evans for her diligent review of the criminal justice chapter. Civil attorneys William Shernoff,

Charles Lipcon, and Doug Roberts, as well as Fred Beck of Alliance of American Insurers, Ralph Jackson of Allstate, and Bob Plunk of Preferred Risk Mutual, all deserve appreciation for their consultation regarding financial recovery for victims. David Flowers and Jim Reynolds of Gandy, Michiner, Swindle, Whittaker, Pratt, and Mercer in Fort Worth, Texas were especially helpful, as was financial planner, Jerry Cosby.

While a multitude of victims were remembered and quoted in the book, special thanks go to Janet Barton, Greg Novak, Bob and Pat Preston, Ralph Shelton, Betty Jane Spencer, and Howard Velzey, for reading the manuscript in whole and offering constructive criticism.

The second edition was greatly enhanced by the addition of the chapter on suicide and for that I am grateful for the encouragement and assistance of Anne Seymour. With the assistance of colleague Stephanie Frogge, additions were made to the "Brother or Sister" chapter in the fourth edition.

Mothers Against Drunk Driving made the project possible by allowing me time to write. The national staff and board as well as the MADD chapters have been more than supportive of my work for the last eight years. Without that, the book would have been no more than a dream.

Finally, I respect and appreciate immeasurably my publisher and editor, Eugene Wheeler, who has labored with me as a true colleague, attending victim conferences and speaking with victims to gain for himself a better feel of the victim experience. His wife, Genie, became committed to the project as well and has been a treasured source of support throughout.

And so, I launch *No Time for Goodbyes* fourth edition, with the hope that it will touch the hearts and minds of those who do not deserve to feel alone or without hope. May their grieving and growing be a fitting memorial to the spirits of those whom they have loved.

Janice Harris Lord

July, 1991

# CONTENTS

# PREFACE

Before beginning my work with homicide survivors, I thought I was accustomed to the aftermath of violence. I had worked with children who had been physically abused and sexually molested. I had counseled battered women. I thought I had witnessed the pinnacle of rage, the depths of despair. I was naive.

In 1983, I became Director of Victim Services at the national headquarters of Mothers Against Drunk Driving. During the first week of phone calls and letters from victims, I realized that grieving the loss of a loved one who had been killed suddenly, violently, and senselessly is unique.

I met Mary Anna Downing, whose son, Eddie, had been killed by a drunk driver a year and a half before, and whose son, Jimmy, had just been killed by another drunk driver. I attended Jimmy's funeral and saw him lowered into the ground beside his brother whose grave was still without grass or tombstone. My mind spun in the awareness that Mary Anna Downing would now have to buy headstones for two children, would have to deal with four insurance companies, and would be thrust into two separate criminal justice systems with a myriad of players. A school cafeteria worker, Mary Anna supplemented her income by selling Avon products. She was now too devastated to do either. I wondered how she would survive.

I later met Carl and Mary Mittag. Still grieving the loss of Mary's father to cancer, they now faced the sudden killing of her mother, aunt, and cousin while vacationing in Florida. I witnessed their agony in coping not only with grief but with frustrations about criminal justice, wrongful death civil suits, and insurance settlements—all in states far from their home.

The criminal trial resulted in a verdict of "not guilty" for the driver, although he was clearly intoxicated. Two years later, the wrongful death suits were still pending and not one cent of insurance money had been paid to the survivors.

As I expanded my attention to other homicide survivors, I met Betty Jane Spencer, whose four sons were shot and killed in an execution-style massacre in their rural Indiana home. Betty Jane was wounded but survived. As she looks back on it she says, "I was killed too. I just didn't die."

Betty Jane still carries a gun and doesn't sleep well when she is alone in her home. Out of the ashes of her experience, however, she kindled multiple legislative changes for victim rights in Indiana and has been a source of strength to many victims who lean on her. She is now State Administrator of MADD, Florida.

If you comment on her strength, she says, "No, I'm not strong. I do have courage though." Her definition of courage came from John Wayne: "Courage is being afraid and saddling up anyway."

I have conducted support groups in which everyone present was grieving the death of someone they loved to a violent, senseless act. I have seen in these groups the wonderful healing power of a fellow struggler who can honestly say, "I understand something of what you feel because I've walked in your shoes."

Even though my understanding is limited by not being a victim myself, I have acquired some insights which may help homicide survivors to cope. Many of them come from the survivors themselves. This book is not a scholarly report on grief research, although I have read and participated in many studies. It will, however, heighten the awareness of professionals about the homicide survivor experience.

This book focuses on needs of family and friends of some-one loved who has been killed. It informs them that what they are experiencing is normal, based on the degree of trauma they have been through. It makes practical suggestions for coming to grips with grief and for coping with the systems with which they will be forced to interact.

It is written to help family and friends know that they will, with time and effort, feel better than they do now. Some homicide survivors may not yet be ready to feel better. They are so focused on the one who has been killed that they do not want to focus on themselves. They will in time. When they are ready, their burden may be lightened because they will find in these pages that they are not alone.

This book is written in the spirit of a man whose mother, father, wife, and brother were murdered in the Holocaust, and who said:

...*Everything can be taken from a man but one thing: the freedom to choose one's attitude in any given set of circumstances*...

Viktor Frankl

*Man's Search for Meaning*[1]

1 Frankl, Victor, *Man's Search for Meaning: An Introduction to Logotherapy*, New York: Washington Square Press, 1963 (p. 104).

# I

## YOUR GRIEF IS UNIQUE

Pain too deep for words may be your experience now. Or that kind of pain may be a vivid memory. Someone you loved has been killed violently, perhaps in a vehicular crash or a freak accident of some sort, perhaps murdered.

Death is probably not new to you. You may have previously experienced the deaths of others whom you have loved. But now you may wonder why you are having so much difficulty "handling" this death.

During your lifetime you may have lost family members and friends as a result of a terminal illness or old age. Death is never easy for those who are left behind. However, most human beings recover, and, in time, memories of the "good times" replace memories of the grief of the final days.

The sudden, violent death which took your loved one probably feels very unlike other losses you have experienced. You may be angrier than you have ever been and sadder than you thought possible. You may have frightening thoughts. You may do strange things. You may be afraid you are "going crazy."

Don't be alarmed. Few people deeply in grief "go crazy." Getting through your misery can be so devastating, though, that you begin to question your own sanity.

Most people can accept the fact that "accidents" happen. But a sudden accident is more difficult to cope with than an expected death. It is even more traumatic if it came both suddenly and violently. In criminal victimization, the fact that someone **chose** to be negligent, or selected a victim to brutalize, cannot be assimilated by those who are left behind. It makes no sense at all.

Second victimizations can injure survivors as they become rejected by family and friends for what happened, or when services or programs designed to help them are found lacking due to callousness.

Families are never prepared for the fact that a loved one can be killed suddenly and violently. Nor are they prepared to face weeks, months, and even years of waiting until a criminal case is resolved and insurance claims and civil suits are settled. During this period, people counted on for support fail them. Unfortunately, many of those who attempt to comfort survivors, and even some professionals who should know better, don't understand that grieving following the traumatic stress of homicide will be intense and long-lasting.

Studies seeking to understand grieving have been conducted for years. While trends are fairly predictable about "grief cycles," the strongest conclusion reached is that each person grieves differently, although not so differently that sufferers of similar losses can't understand and share each others' grief journeys.

**How you grieve depends on a number of things:**

- The way you learned to cope with stress in your life before this tragedy;
- The quality of the relationship you had with the person who was killed;
- The circumstances under which your loved one was killed;
- The success you have dealing with the criminal justice system, insurance companies, and the myriad of other systems you must face in the aftermath of your tragedy;
- Your religious beliefs and ethnic customs; and
- The emotional support your family and friends offer while you are grieving.

It is amazing but true that a few people handle trauma well. They bounce back to a fulfilling life soon after their loved one dies. Most of these people have strong support from their family and friends and a healthy supply of good memories about the one who died. However, most families in which someone has been killed have a very difficult time with it.

## Anticipated Death

Let us look for a moment at what we know about grief following death which is anticipated and non-violent. Doing so will help us understand the uniqueness of homicide. It is tempting to label anticipated and non-violent death as "normal," but few people in grief, even in the best of circumstances, feel "normal." However, the griever who is fortunate enough to know ahead of time that death is approaching may react differently than you do.

When people learn that a loved one is likely to die, they may not believe it at first. They may seek several medical opinions to be sure—and rightly so.

As they begin to believe that death really is forthcoming, they may get angry—angry that modern science can develop machines as miraculous as computers, but can't find a cure for particular diseases. They may be angry at God for allowing

3

death. They may pray fervently for God to intervene, and then feel frustrated if God doesn't seem to answer their prayers.

They may be sad and depressed as they face the fact that their loved one will die. They may long for relief for their loved one as they see the body deteriorate.

If, however, family and friends are able to accept the fact that death is coming, and the one who is dying has reached a degree of acceptance, they will have the opportunity to express their feelings, resolve problems, and relate lovingly and honestly during the last days.

Even in the best of circumstances, though, survivors are often surprised to learn that they will go through many of the same feelings of disbelief, anger, and sadness after the death. It seems to be a part of human nature that emotionally healthy human beings resist death, their own as well as someone else's, and that is probably as it should be.

Knowing that death is approaching can bring people closer together or it may cause them to distance themselves emotionally. Either way, it is believed to cushion the impact of the death when it comes. Coming to grips with an anticipated death usually takes from three to twenty-four months, according to most research. In some cases it can take years. Most people find that if they "lean in" to grieving, allow their emotions to flow, and talk openly about their loss, they will, little by little, be cleansed of much of the pain. Those who attempt to deny their grief and pretend that nothing has happened may have more difficulty.

## Traumatic Death

Your experience may be quite unlike what has just been described because death came to your loved one suddenly. You had no time to say "good-bye," "I'm sorry," or "I love you."

*The sad part is that she died alone. There were no last "I love you's," or "Thank you's," or "Hey, I really appreciate all you do's." There were no soft smiles, no caring words—only screams. Screams that echoed through the empty chambers of my mind where laughter once reigned.*

> Tammy Luke. Written in memory of her friend Laura Porter

## Violence of the Death

The death your loved one faced may have been violent. Perhaps his or her body was mutilated. That fact may be more painful for you than it was for the loved one who was killed.

When people are seriously injured, they usually go into shock and never experience pain. Many who have recovered say that it was some time before they felt pain, even if they drifted in and out of consciousness. Most do not remember the point of impact, whether it was from an automobile crash, a gunshot wound, or other form of trauma.

Therefore, the shock to you, the survivor, upon learning of the tragedy may have been more terrifying than that of the one who died. Even so, you would have done anything to prevent your loved one's body from being violated.

Human beings have personalities, and most people believe they have spirits or souls. But bodies are also important. You grieve the loss of your loved one's personality and spirit, but you also grieve the loss of his or her living body. You saw it. You touched it. It touched you. You miss it.

5

## TO MY DEAD DAUGHTER

*Fair daughter, sister, friend and heart-mate;*
*soul's child, Eros, muse and mirror.*

*I kissed the arching feet,*
*the small cold hands, the purpled lids.*
*A drop of blood from your smooth brow*
*I licked, like any mother beast,*
*mewing, nuzzling, howling*
*over its cub.*
*Mad with pain*
*I stroke your body—-heavy now—-*
*that had such lightness, grace,*
*its gold warmth now yellowing.*
*No. This is not you!*
*You are not here.*

*I search, my darling, everywhere.*
*My stunned feet grope forest paths.*
*Through shared waters my body moves.*
*I float upon your river of dark hair.*
*Are you there?*
*I grasp the air.*

Anita Huffington. Written
in memory of her daughter

You not only miss the living presence and body of your loved one, but you may deeply resent the fact that it was not respected by the killer. You may feel guilty at not being able to protect your loved one, even if you know it was not possible.

Because of the condition of your loved one's body, you may not have been able to view it at the hospital or funeral home. If this was the case, you now rely on fantasies to form a picture of how you think he or she looked.

6

You may doubt that your loved one actually died. You may find yourself expecting him or her to walk through the door or call on the telephone at any minute. Most survivors feel this way for awhile, but it may be even more vivid if you were unable to see your loved one's body.

Most people who were able to view their loved one are glad they did. If you were unable to do so, you may have to find other ways to assure yourself of the reality of the death.

*Michael was so badly battered—many head injuries. I refused to let his three younger brothers go into the hospital room. I regret that now. In an effort to spare them, I robbed them of their last chance to see their brother alive.*

*Even though the casket was closed to the public, our family did get to see and touch his body before the funeral. His brother James, 15, slipped Mike's graduation key and tassel in his breast pocket before we closed the casket.*

Rita Chiavacci, whose son Michael, age 19, was killed.

Funeral Directors are encouraged to allow surviving family members as much choice as possible about viewing bodies. Most loved ones know what they can handle. If the funeral director will describe what the body will look like, survivors can be counted on to make the choice about viewing that is right for them.

Funeral Directors are also encouraged to take photos of the deceased in their final state so that if family members choose not to view immediately, but wish to look at the photos weeks, months, or years later, they may.

Other options exist for those who, for whatever reason, did not view the body. Law enforcement agencies, fire departments, medical examiner's offices, and District Attorney offices frequently have photographs. Because some of these photos are stark and graphic, agencies are often reluctant to allow families to see them. They believe that their refusal is compassionate. You may need to be assertive in your request.

Parents of Murdered Children recommends a procedure for viewing pictures that many have found useful. The person wishing to view the photos should take their closest support person (which may or may not be a spouse). Ask the keeper of the photos to place each one in a separate envelope and arrange them with the least offensive photo on top and the most offensive photo on bottom. Show the first photo to the support person. The survivor then has two sources of data: the description of the photo which the support person can offer, and the affect of the support person as he or she looked at the photo. On the basis of that, a decision can be made about looking or not looking. Many times, only one or two photos will be viewed, but survivors may wish to take copies of the others home to view when they are ready. They should have that choice if the criminal justice case is complete and there is no longer a legal need for securing the photos within the agency.

Viewing bodies at the scene of the crime is a similar issue. Once emergency medical care has been administered and the crime scene has been properly recorded by the law enforcement agency, survivors should be allowed to make a choice about seeing, touching, or holding the body of their loved one. Attendants should be very clear in describing the condition of the body, so that the choice is an informed one. Again, most people know what they can and can't handle. Very rarely does a survivor report regret that they were allowed to go to their loved one's body. Most are grateful that they did. Hospitals have changed policies rapidly within the last few years to allow presence and touch through the death experience and for as long as family members wish to stay following the death.

In some cases, the body is discovered by a loved one before support services arrive. Victims of murder are often found by a family member. Vehicular crashes are sometimes witnessed by family or friends. Shock, numbness, and rage are normal re-

8

sponses to such a violent scene. The visual imprint of the death scene can be overwhelming and long lasting.

Professional counselors can help persons who are fixated on the death scene to diffuse the impact of the violence. This is accomplished through emotional support as the experience is discussed, and techniques are used to help recall the memory with less horror. With help, positive memories of the loved one will replace the distressing images.

## Untimeliness of the Death

A sudden death is never timely. Whether the one killed was your child, mate, parent, brother or sister, or even your friend, the shock can be devastating.

### Your Child

If your child was killed, a part of you feels aborted too. Your parental drive to nurture and protect may be there, but it now has nowhere to go. A child's death feels terribly wrong. You expected to pre-decease your child. It doesn't seem right that this natural pattern should be reversed. This is true whether the one killed was a young child or an adult child. Your child is always your child.

*"No! You're lying—*
*It can't be!" I screamed*
*as I ran about pounding my head.*
*"I'm sorry," the officer replied,*
*"but your son didn't make it.*
*He's dead."*
*"Oh, dear God, how can it be?"*
*I cried.*
*"He was just a kid of seventeen!"*

Florence (Mickey) Mikalauskas. Written in memory of her son.

9

## Your Mate

If your mate was killed, you may have suddenly lost your best friend, your lover, your co-parent, a bread-winner, and your main confidant. Being forced to make major decisions alone, to maintain the family, and to grieve, all at the same time, can be devastating.

*At 7:30 a.m., my wife died with me at her side. But I never saw her conscious. I have nightmares about that moment even still. I feel I let her down. I wish I could have just looked into her eyes once and said, "I Love You."*

*Our second Christmas without Michelle is now approaching. There are no words to explain the grief that I and our three children, Erika, 7, Kimberly, 5, and Jeffrey, 2, have gone through this past year. The two girls still have nightmares. Jeffrey never knew his mother. How can I explain a broken heart and broken dreams?*

> Joseph Lawrence, whose
> 35 year-old wife was killed.

## Your Parent

If your parent was killed, no matter how old he or she was, you deeply regret that the death was undignified. Many will say, "He lived a good, full life," but it feels wrong that you could not say "thank you for giving me life" or "goodbye," or "I'm sorry that your death came violently."

*February 11, 1982, was a very long day*
*—the longest. My mother's surprise*
*visit turned into tragedy. Now, two*
*days later, eyes red, I'm sitting on*
*an airplane flying my mother's body home.*

*How do you say to your brothers, "Mom is dead—killed in a needless crash?*

*I had a rough year and, as always, Mom was coming to comfort me. Now, this is Mom's last flight home to Iowa. It was so quick— so unnecessary—I miss her so much I can hardly bear it.*

Barbara Brodt

## Your Sibling

If your brother or sister was killed, you may feel guilty at being alive, even though it doesn't make rational sense. Siblings are often alike. Because a sibling's death can remind you of your own mortality, it is especially difficult to face. If your brother or sister could be killed in an instant, so could you. Sometimes the pain the death of a sibling has brought to your family can make you conclude that the wrong child died.

*Dale, I'm just so glad for the time we had together. And I'm glad we were close. But I'm so sad and so sorry we won't have any more laughter or good times together. I will always love you and I will never, ever stop missing you. I just pray that no other brother or sister will have to feel the way I feel now. There is an empty space inside of me that can't ever be filled again. No one can take your place.*

Written by Debra Mumblo, whose brother was killed.

## Senselessness of the Death

Another difficult component of grieving the death of your loved one is the senselessness of it. You can understand when

11

bodies wear out with age or when diseases can't be cured. But violent deaths are intentional or a result of negligence. They are someone's fault.

Many murderers have been in a prison or mental hospital and would still be there if the system had worked effectively. You don't understand why society doesn't protect us from such people.

Most vehicular crashes are caused by someone who chose to be irresponsible. Over half are caused by drunk drivers. Most involve speeding. Many are caused by people who refuse to stop and rest and then fall asleep behind the wheel. Most crashes could have been prevented.

One of the most difficult losses for survivors is a murder in which the offender was known—the babysitter who kills a child, the teenager who kills his date, the jealous lover who kills the "ex," the drunk driver who kills one of his own family members.

If you know the offender, your mind may be in turmoil with confusing and conflicting feelings. You may feel guilty because you didn't intervene sooner. It is difficult to blame someone you know. You may worry about what will happen to the offender in the criminal and civil justice systems. Knowing that your loved one's death could have been prevented may be one of the most painful aspects of your grieving.

## Criminal Justice Frustrations

Because most violent deaths lead to involvement with the criminal justice system, you will no doubt feel frustrated as you face procedures you don't understand. You may not understand why the State can require an autopsy. You may be left out of meetings and hearings that mean the world to you. You may expect to be informed and involved in all critical stages of the criminal case, but you will not be unless you are assertive.

12

*I contacted the District Attorney's office about two months after my children were killed. I was given the impression that my presence and questions were an imposition to the Assistant DA handling the case. To me, my children were human beings—not just reports lying on someone's desk.*

*Was it wrong for me, their mother, to want to see that the man who had killed my children was prosecuted?*

*I was not told when the trial would be held and found out only when it appeared in the newspaper. I wasn't allowed to be in the courtroom because my "presence" might bias the jury. Yet the offender was present through the entire trial. The jury never even saw **pictures** of my beautiful children—and they never knew who I was as I sat alone in the hall the three days of the trial.*

> Mary Mitchell, whose children, Bart, 5, and Gayla, 7, were killed.

## Financial Stress

Your financial security may now be threatened. Emergency medical care and funerals cost money. You probably missed several days or weeks of work. You may have difficulty concentrating when at work. That may threaten your job security. You may have hired a special investigator to ensure ample evidence for prosecution and a civil suit. You may have paid for the travel of relatives to come to the funeral. All of that takes money.

## Faith/Philosophy of Life Issues

Even if you've never pondered about "life," "death," or "God" before, you probably are thinking about them now. Or, you may have previously thought a lot about them and thought you had them all figured out. Now, none of your ideas work. Your theories are topsy turvy. This sense of alienation from what made sense before can cause you to despair. It will take time

13

and effort to reconstruct your basic beliefs to accommodate this tragedy.

## Summary

I have not painted a pretty picture. Your loss was sudden and unanticipated. It was violent. It was senseless and unnecessary. It was untimely. It may have plunged you into a criminal justice system which is difficult to understand. You may now be under financial stress. And, you may be struggling to develop a faith or philosophy of life which works for you.

It is not the purpose of this book to bewilder you or perplex you. Its purpose is to help you understand why your grief may not be like other types of grief you have read about. It is to help you understand why you feel angry when others tell you, three months after your loss, that you should "get on with your life."

Don't be alarmed if you cry while reading this book. That only means that you need to cry. Grieving involves crying. It is painful, but it is healthy. Most people feel some release from pain after crying because it helps them get in touch with parts of themselves they couldn't touch in any other way.

Understanding more about the uniqueness of your grief will not change how you feel about your loved one, but it may enable you to feel more comfortable about yourself. It may enable you, also, to take what others say with a grain of salt if their expectations of you do not fit with your own grieving experience.

# II

## GRIEF FOLLOWING TRAGEDY

Like everyone else, you are vulnerable to deep emotional reactions following trauma. These reactions are normal responses to a very abnormal event.

The kind of person you were before your loved one was killed will make a difference in how you react. If you are physically healthy and emotionally healthy, had a good relationship with your loved one, have a supportive network of friends, feel basically in control of your life, and tend to see crises as challenges rather than catastrophes, you will handle the trauma of having a loved one killed better than those who are not so fortunate.

No matter how "all-together" you are, however, recovering from a traumatic and unexpected death will require a lot of patience and a lot of work. You will never be exactly the same again.

**Getting better means:**
- Solving problems and completing tasks in your daily work routine again,
- Sleeping well and having energy again,

15

- Feeling good enough about yourself to be hopeful about your present and your future,
- Being able to enjoy the pleasurable and beautiful things in life.

You probably will be able to achieve these in time. For most people it takes months, even years. Current research shows that the bereavement period following a sudden death is intense for three to four years and is never complete.

You will never forget what happened. If you are afraid to get better because you think you might forget your loved one, stop worrying about that. You will never forget. You will always cherish the memory of your loved one. You will always be sorry you didn't share life with him or her for many more years. However, in time, you will remember the happy memories more easily than the painful ones which fill your mind now.

## Stage Theories

People have been writing about "stages" as long as they have been talking about death and crime victimization, including the sudden death of homicide. Most of us know about Elizabeth Kubler-Ross' stages: denial, anger, bargaining, depression, and acceptance. Her research was based primarily on both adults and children and their families who were facing death in the near future. Marton Bard and Dawn Sangrey are early pioneers in research about crime victimization. They refer to initial disorganization/shock, struggle/recoil, and readjustment. Dr. Therese Rando, one of our country's finest contemporary grief researchers, speaks of three stages: avoidance, confrontation, and re-establishment.

Stages are fine as long as we understand them as the researchers do - that they are **not** firm, concrete, and predictable. They offer broad trends which may make you feel more normal as you read about them. Just be sure that you understand them as **descriptive**, not **prescriptive**. They become **prescriptive** when they cause you to believe that you are not "grieving properly" if you do not fit into the mold. Over-emphasis on stages overlooks the totality of life. You come to your trauma very much a

16

different person from someone else in some other town who experienced a trauma similar to yours. Your daily life differs. The "stage" you're in may not vary by month, but by hour; and is certainly affected by whom you are with at any given time.

So, be gentle and patient with yourself as you learn about stages. And, as you later reach out to help others, remember that it is harmful to try to push people from one stage to another. It's easy to think that "denial" or "shock" represents character weakness and that people should "face what happened."

A mental health professional who should have known better said, "I really don't like being around you while you're in your angry stage. Go home and get through that, and when you get depressed, come back and we'll do something about that."

## Components of Response to Sudden Death

The following components are not "stages." They are pieces of the grief experience that most survivors experience from time to time or many times.

### Denial/Shock/Numbness

Denial is a wonderful thing. It is nature's way of warding off the full impact of trauma until you can absorb it. Most people, upon being told that a loved one has been killed, are rendered literally too weak to undertake the overwhelming task of grieving.

You may have gone into shock. Going into shock is something like being given a general anesthetic. With the help of a quick spurt of adrenalin, your initial response may have been "fight" or "flight" or "freeze." Fighters sometimes physically attack the person who has delivered the bad news. Police officers who deliver death notifications say this is common. Those whose reaction is "flight" may faint or run to escape the pain. "Frozen fright" describes those unable to react.

*It was 12:30 am on June 10th when the call came from the hospital telling me that my son, John, had been injured. Because I was alone, the police came to pick me up. All the way to Massachusetts General, the two officers in front talked about trivial matters. Neither of them spoke a word to me. When we got to the hospital, I was questioned about insurance and then put in a room by myself.*

*I sat alone reciting the Hail Mary aloud to break the silence and tension. Eventually, a young doctor, obviously tired and aggravated, entered the room, hopped up on a gurney, and said, "Your son has expired." That's all.*

*"I don't know what to say," I stammered, as if I could ever be prepared for such an event. I ran from the hospital, and outside, screamed, and screamed, and screamed.*

> Margaret Grogan, whose son, John, was stabbed in the heart at a graduation party.

*I prayed all the way to the hospital, "Please God, at least give him five more minutes." But it was too late. Since I'm a registered nurse, I've had to tell people that their child was dead. It's something that you never get used to. But I never dreamed I would walk into an emergency room and have my husband tell me, "Oh God, Sally, our baby is dead." I watched a nice man dissolve before my eyes. I felt my 15 year-old son hitting on me, begging me to say his brother wasn't dead. I watched my daughter crumble and say, "Mom, I want to get the guy who did this."*

> Sally Jeanes, whose 18 year-old son, Jason, was killed by a drunk driver.

Regardless of the initial impact, if you are like most people, you soon found yourself in a state of numbness. Looking back on it now, you may wonder how you remained calm. You may have completed some tasks which now seem impossible. You probably have a hard time remembering exactly what you did during those first few days.

> *I was having trouble making sense of it and nurses were staring at me. I didn't want to think about the boys and what had happened to them. I was alive. Maybe they were too.*
>
> *Words seemed to hang in the air while I tried to make sense of them. Words like "dead" and "autopsy" floated through. I didn't want to hear them. But all I could say was, "Please don't tell me how many are dead."*
>
> Betty Jane Spencer recalling her condition before being told that her four sons had been killed.

During this time, people may have commented on how "strong" you were. One of the saddest parts of trauma is that people assume you are strong when you really are in shock. You may appear strong, but you feel like a mechanical robot. When the shock wears off and you desperately need your friends, they have resumed life as usual, believing that you are doing fine.

> *For the first few months I was in a daze. I was plagued by flashbacks, but I only half believed it was real. Friends commented on how brave and calm and strong I was. What they did not know was that I had not yet fully comprehended the enormity of what had happened.*
>
> Barbara Kaplan who was seriously injured, but survived a shooting in which two of her friends were killed.

Denial following a violent and unanticipated loss should be considered normal and functional. You should be allowed to travel through this part of grief at your own pace, because denial will serve you well until you are stronger and better able to cope. It is impossible to push through any part of grieving in order to "get it over with." If you cannot think clearly, seem forgetful, and seem detached, be patient with yourself. If you need help, ask for it. However, be **very** careful about use of alcohol and prescriptive drugs. They only push you into an **un**natural denial. Your own body is compensating for the trauma. Let it.

### Fear/Vulnerability

Many survivors are surprised to find that they feel anxious, fearful, and powerless in the aftermath of a killing. Even though you knew that tragedies happened, they happened to other people. Before your trauma, you felt uniquely invulnerable. It wouldn't happen to you.

After your loved one was killed, you may have felt that life was "out of kilter." It's strange how we tend to believe that good things happen to good people and bad things happen to bad people. That belief, for you, is now proven false.

You may feel that you and your remaining loved ones are more vulnerable than others. That's frightening. You will need to think rationally and work hard to risk going out even when it frightens you. Little by little, you can overcome these fears. It is maddening to realize that the killer not only destroyed your loved one, but also damaged the part of you that was previously confident and carefree.

*The fact that I could be killed hit me with full force. I felt powerless and off-balance. Would I feel frightened of everyone I didn't know?....I saw each stranger as a potential killer. I envied those who walked trusting others. I worried about becoming weak and fearful.*

Jean Goldberg

*If you think about it, everything we do in life depends on others acting in a rational and predictable way. When you get in a car and drive it away, you're investing a lot of trust in every other driver on the road. So what happens when that trust is gone? Try driving down a two-lane highway with cars passing you just a few feet over in the oncoming lane. Your guts will be in knots if you can handle it at all. When you start to see every faceless stranger as a potential madman or thug, you're not only scared, but depressed. You really feel betrayed!*

Barbara Kaplan

*Since that week I feel differently about life. I don't feel so young. I'm 27, but after losing my 4 year-old son, I know there's nothing fair about death. I often think it could happen again. I think of death often. I told my mother the other day that I'll miss her when she dies.*

Kim Keyes, whose child, Kurt, was killed in an automobile crash along with three other relatives and a family friend.

The fear and vulnerability of now knowing that tragedy can strike anyone at anytime has an almost existential quality. It leads to questions like, "What is life, anyhow?" "What are we here for?" "Why do people have to die?" "Why didn't God do something to stop it?" These issues can be doubly overwhelming to adolescents who are only beginning to try to figure out life, let alone death. Facing the pain in the household can be so overwhelming that youth sometimes seek ways to escape rather than face their own vulnerability.

**Physical Symptoms**

Stress following trauma can make you physically sick. As you experience sadness, confusion, fear, anxiety, and anger, you may find that you have no appetite. You may feel weak, as if you couldn't take another step. You may feel exhausted, but when you go to bed you can't sleep or you sleep only a short time. Your sex drive may be gone or diminished.

Many survivors speak of pain, stomach aches, heaviness in their chest—a symptom some refer to as "a broken heart." You may feel nervous and edgy.

Some survivors begin to think of suicide as these symptoms escalate. They wish they could die too, to escape the pain. Friends and relatives who care are critical to your well-being at these times.

You may need help in thinking rationally about what is best for you and your family.

You may need to see a doctor, especially if you are not eating or not sleeping. The immune system of most people in grief loses some of its effectiveness. This may cause you to be more vulnerable to disease.

People in grief may also be accident prone. Many are involved in automobile accidents, falls, or other mishaps. These can happen because you are preoccupied with your loss.

If you are vulnerable to cardiovascular disease or other serious illnesses, you need to have regular checkups. Some research has suggested a correlation between grief and the onset of cancer.

If you use tobacco or drugs including alcohol, you will need to very carefully monitor your use of them. Some people in grief increase their usage in order to escape and to sleep. This only leads to more serious problems.

Alcohol is a depressant. It will increase rather than decrease your grief. It will also aggravate other physical conditions. Grieving, as painful as it is, is usually best leaned into and fully experienced. Alcohol and other drugs will not really help. They may prolong your grief.

You may need short term medication prescribed by your doctor to help you eat or sleep while grieving. If so, do not consider it a weakness. You have suffered severe trauma and deserve professional help to begin feeling better. You will probably need the help of prescribed drugs only for a short time. Even if you don't want to feel better yet, you owe it to yourself and your family to stay in good health.

**Anger**

You may be surprised at the intensity of anger you feel for the person who killed your loved one. The more senseless the act, the more angry you may become. Some survivors don't feel angry, but most do—even to the point of rage.

> *I didn't think it was possible to hate someone so much. I felt the most deep penetrating hate I have ever known in my life. I'm a pastor and it's pretty shocking to find out the kinds of feelings one can have.*
>
> Tinka Bloedow whose 14 year-old daughter, Tee Ja, was killed by a drunk driver.

You may wish desperately that the person who killed your loved one would show some remorse, say "I'm sorry." That probably won't happen.

Many offenders do not feel remorse. Some are indeed sorry. Their attorneys, however, will warn them to make no contact with the victim family because such contact can be considered an admission of guilt.

You may have felt angry early in your grieving or later, after some of the numbness wore off. You may have felt angry before you were willing to admit it.

23

It is unfortunate that most of us were taught as children that some feelings are bad. Most of us heard:

- "You shouldn't get angry."
- "It's wrong to feel jealous."
- "It's sinful to feel vengeance."
- "Rage is a terrible thing."

Feelings are not right or wrong. They simply are. Your behavior may be good or bad, right or wrong, appropriate or not appropriate. Your thinking may be clear or foggy, rational or irrational.

But your feelings are simply your feelings with no "shoulds" attached. It is silly of people to suggest that you should stop having a particular feeling. It is impossible.

*It might comfort victims, especially those who feel cheated by the criminal justice system, to know that it is acceptable and helpful to fantasize about the "justice" they would impose on the killer.*

*One of the most helpful things I learned in coping was that feelings are involuntary—like the urge to sneeze— and can seldom be suppressed. Even the most negative of angry thoughts and feelings are not wrong. "Wrong" comes in only if they translate into behaviors.*

Janet Barton, whose son
was murdered

It is very important that you not act destructively in response to your feelings of anger. You must force yourself to think rationally about what you will do with your anger. But what you feel is what you feel.

You may find that you are angry, not just at the person who killed your loved one, but at God, the doctors, the investigating officers, the people you love very much—your family. You may be angry at everyone who seems to be going on with life as if nothing happened. You may even be angry at your dead loved one for abandoning you, no matter how much you know it wasn't his or her fault. Obviously, such anger is misplaced, and should not be acted out.

> *And there is anger. My anger didn't stop at God or at the murderers. I hated everything and everyone. It was a raw, ugly, destructive feeling that could rise in me and control me for days on end.*
>
> Betty Jane Spencer, whose four sons were murdered.

The injustice of your loved one's death, the deep hurt you feel, and the loss of future dreams may all add up to rage—a wordless drive to do something. Most of the things you think about doing must remain undone—like killing the offender.

> *I fantasized for a year about going into the courtroom and blowing his head off. But I decided to leave it all in God's hands. Things have a way of turning out.*
>
> June Sanborn, whose only child Diane, was murdered by choking, stabbing, and sexual mutilation.

It's okay to think about it, and it's very helpful to talk about it with someone who is willing to listen. If you can find someone who has felt the same way with whom to share your feelings, you are very fortunate.

Many friends will not be willing to hear you ventilate these intense feelings. That's sad. Their response may also make you more angry. It would be nice if they could understand that, in

25

expressing them, you are taking responsibility for them, and are not likely to act on them.

Allowing yourself to express the feelings will probably free your mind, enabling you to be more open and realistic in your thinking and planning for the future.

One of the components of anger is its physical manifestations. If you suppress it—try to stop yourself from feeling it—you may develop problems in your body. Symptoms can include headaches, stomach aches, colitis, backaches, high blood pressure and others.

On the other hand, doing something physical often helps. Some people run, exercise vigorously, or clean house. Others write—in journals, in letters to the offender (which are usually best unmailed). Some cry and yell and scream.

What you do with your anger really doesn't matter as long as you admit that it's there and don't hurt yourself or anyone else in expressing it.

You may find that your anger is serving a somewhat useful purpose. Lurking beneath the anger you may find deep sadness. Even though anger doesn't feel good, it is usually less painful than sadness. Anger can either be focused on someone else or it can be directed in a wide spectrum, not seeming to attach to anyone or anything for long. Sadness is focused inside yourself. You will eventually need to give up some of the anger, rage, and vengeance to experience what's underneath it.

When you decide to discover what's beneath the anger, you may find gut-wrenching agony. By being willing to face it, you may find some relief from your anger. You may think that you owe it to your loved one to remain angry. That doesn't make a lot of sense. But what you do with your anger and when you decide to look beneath it are up to you.

This somewhat confused society of ours seems to be telling us in print, on television, and in the movies that anger must be ventilated at all cost. Research is not finding that to be so. In fact, those who spend much of their lives spewing anger are those who are **more** likely than others to get sick. The **goal** is to get what you want, not just to ventilate.

As someone recently said, "If blowing your stack pollutes the air, you're not going to win!"

You may hear that the prosecutor is contemplating a plea bargain which you don't understand and that he has no plan to consult you about it. That's enough to enrage you!! But, the question is, "How can I get what I want?" Throwing a fit in the prosecutor's office or writing a nasty "letter to the editor" is more likely to alienate than to get what you want.

Call the prosecutor and ask for a **fifteen minute** appointment to discuss the case. Calmly ask why he is considering the plea rather than pushing for the original charges. Sometimes, there is a very good reason. In several states now, second-degree murder is being charged in serious drunk driving death cases. The legal elements required to accomplish a second-degree murder conviction are complex. Perhaps, as the investigation is carried out, not all the necessary elements can be proven. In such a case, it might be better to accept a guilty plea to the lesser offense than to risk losing everything. If it's a judgement call, you may want to proceed to trial. You may be willing to risk losing in order to risk winning. Many prosecutors will take your wishes into consideration, even though they do retain ultimate discretion in the decision. Some won't because they don't want to risk acquittals on their record. But you will probably feel a lot better after discussing your "hurt" about what you "heard" than if you had acted out your intense rage with the prosecutor.

**Post-Traumatic Stress/Guilt**

For a long time, it was believed that most of the painful stress people feel comes from within. Depressed people were thought to have serious internal conflicts which needed to be worked out.

Now, we understand that external trauma is also a valid basis for continuing distress. While this understanding may or may not help you feel better, it is good news. It is good news because it means that you are not "crazy" just because you are experiencing very painful symptoms as a result of your loved one's death.

As denial and shock wear off, you may experience some feelings which are foreign to you—and frightening. You may find that particular memories of your trauma keep intruding into your mind. They may be particular sights or sounds. You may have nightmares over and over again. Something may make you feel as if the trauma were happening again. If you are aware of what the trigger is—perhaps the scene of the death, a certain song, certain events—you may almost compulsively avoid the trigger, somewhat like a phobia.

You may feel that the external world doesn't have much meaning anymore. You may feel like withdrawing because it seems that no one understands your pain. You may have difficulty concentrating, and become absentminded and confused.

### THE MOTHER LODE

*A single eye blazing in my forehead,*
*I mine your death.*
*Sifting through the layers,*
*hording every glint.*

*Here,*
*a pile of undone dreams.*
*And here,*
*a mound of guilt, if onlys,*
*blasted touch.*
*My fossil love.*

*Blackened with loss,*
*deeper and deeper*
*I dig*
*for the mother lode.*

Anita Huffington, written
in memory of her daughter.

28

You may struggle with guilt. For nearly all survivors of a homicide, "If only I had _____," becomes a familiar theme.

Human beings tend to believe a lot of things that don't make sense when examined closely. For instance:

- "People who love each other should always be responsible for each other and be able to protect each other."
- "If I had been a better person, this wouldn't have happened to my loved one."
- "If I begin to feel better it will mean that I didn't love him/her enough."
- "It is not right that my loved one died and I continue to live."
- You may find that when you cry, beneath the tears are the words, "I'm sorry, I'm sorry, I'm sorry."

Perhaps you feel guilty because you still believe the old adage, "Good things happen to good people and bad things happen to bad people." It may seem that if you can just find a way to prove that you were guilty (bad), at least you can hang on to an old belief which makes some sense of your loved one's death.

Possibly the toughest job you will have in grieving is to look **rationally** at why your beliefs make you feel guilty. You may, indeed, be responsible for some component of your loved one's death. If so, acknowledge it and see if you can find a way to forgive yourself. If you made a bad judgement, you probably made the best one you knew how to make at the time. Try not to exaggerate your role because that will confuse you.

In most cases, other factors were largely responsible for your loved one's death. The person who killed your loved one either chose to do so or was negligent in such a way that the death happened, although it was not intentional. Forces of nature also play a role. One law of nature is that when two powerful opposing forces collide, one or both are destroyed. It would be nice, maybe, if such laws did not always work. On the other hand, it would be frightening to live in a world where nature's laws sometimes worked and sometimes didn't.

You may conclude, by thinking rationally, that you were 5% responsible and someone else was 95% responsible. In that case, only take on 5% of the guilt—not 100%.

Talking with others who truly understand what you're going through can help you look at your guilt realistically. It will be hard work for them and for you.

Feeling less guilty won't take away your sadness or your anger, but it can be a big load off our shoulders. It will be worth the effort to rid yourself of it.

## Acknowledgment/Accommodation

The word "acceptance" is not used here because the sudden, violent killing of someone loved is never "acceptable." In the beginning, some feel that they will never be happy again. They go through a period of time when they aren't yet ready to feel better. Others are eager to feel better and work to find ways to do it.

Whether you are ready to feel better or not, you might want to look to others who have survived the ordeal and have managed to regain strength and find happiness again. They can be encouraging models.

It is a fact that your life will not again be the same as it was before your loved one was killed. But it probably will be a lot better than it is now as you read this book.

Acknowledging what happened means believing that it happened as it did, based on all you have learned. It means you no longer have to pretend about it. It means being willing to face and experience the pain rather than avoiding it by over-activism or escape into alcohol or other drugs. It means deciding how to live with your memories. Memories can never be taken from you even though many others will tell you you should forget. Your greater fear is probably forgetting some things you don't want to forget. Many find it helpful to write down six to ten especially wonderful memories. Get them out and read them often. Perhaps with your writings, store a lock of hair, the perfume or aftershave, pieces of clothing, or other mementos. Use these from time to time to cherish the memory. Remind yourself of the good memories when you feel yourself slipping into pain again.

*Accommodation comes when you decide you care whether your own life continues or not. I will never forget Trey, and I will look forward to seeing him in Heaven, but I am going on with my life here, and I find joy in it.*

> Ralph Shelton, Whose son was shot and killed by a sniper.

## Sorrow

You will always feel sorrow that your loved one died tragically and that the long relationship you might have enjoyed was cut short. But sorrow is not the same as the height and width and depth of trauma that most survivors experience for the first months or years. Its parameters are not clear.

Some have described the sorrow as a "misty fog on life" of which you are not always aware. You simply realize that your life is not quite as bright, not quite as light as it was before. Your values have changed. You may be impatient with trivia. You may feel misunderstood. But a sense of sorrow is not the same as being overwhelmed with grief.

*Every time I tell our story, I feel cleansed when it is finished. It's important that people know what a neat kid Kurt was. For the first months, we dwelled on things we didn't do with Kurt. Now we think of things we did do. It's more positive. You need to celebrate what their lives meant to you.*

> Kim Keyes, whose 4 year-old son, Kurt, was killed by a drunk driver.

## Grief Spasms

It is likely that you will experience grief spasms from time to time for years. Survivors are often surprised to find that in the midst of a series of good days, something may bring on a "spasm" of grief. Survivors find anniversaries to be difficult— the birthday of the loved one, the anniversary of the death, the wedding anniversary, Mother's Day, Father's Day. Holidays in which family togetherness is a tradition are often very difficult for families in which someone is now missing. Certain songs can cause a grief spasm. Seeing someone who looks like your loved one can bring on a grief spasm.

Strange as it may seem, though, grief spasms can be understood as celebrations—celebrations of a relationship that meant so much to you that episodes of grief can still overcome you from time to time.

Nearly all survivors are able to say that they would rather have known their loved one as long as they did, than for him or her to have never been born. Being able to experience depths of sadness and heights of joy is to be fully alive, fully human. Most people are glad they are capable of having strong feelings. Having them means that shock symptoms and numbness are no longer necessary and the fullness of the experience of the trauma can be absorbed.

As time goes by, grief spasms will come less frequently and less intensely. Most survivors are able to acknowledge that their loved one would want it that way.

Your loved one would want to be fondly remembered from time to time and even missed. But if the family and friends are caught up in a chronic sense of desperation, the possibility of more set backs could evolve. That would benefit no one and would not be the wish of your loved one.

32

*On some days I'm fine. Then something will happen and I will be right back where I was. I don't cry as much as I did in the beginning. But I don't laugh as much as I did before the crash. Part of me will never come back. But I want it to come back.*

Sally Jeanes, whose 18-year-old son, Jason, was killed.

## Focus on Life

Another component of acknowledgment or "getting better" is an increasing focus on life and a decreasing focus on death. Early on you may have felt that you barely existed. For others to tell you to cheer up and get on with your life seemed to be an unwillingness on their part to share your grief journey. They were uncomfortable and their comfort was more important to them than your discomfort.

You may be disappointed in family and friends for their lack of sensitivity and understanding. It can make you frustrated and angry. However, you will have to decide for yourself when it is right to give more of your attention to living. You can use your grief to continue to drag you down or you can use it to rebuild your life—probably with more compassion and understanding than you had before.

By having experienced trauma, you will be able to look at life and keep it in perspective better than other people. Some survivors seem to have, eventually, a peace and inner wisdom that others lack.

*I feel almost invincible. I have survived the worst thing that could ever happen. All other problems pale in comparison. If I could survive that, I can survive anything.*

Ralph Shelton, whose son was killed by a sniper.

## Call to Justice

In some cases, enduring trauma ignites a spark of activity to right some of the wrongs involved in a sudden violent death. Most survivors want to prevent it for others.

Thousands of men, women, and teenagers have joined Mothers Against Drunk Driving after their loved ones were killed in an effort to help injured victims and survivors cope emotionally, to help them through the criminal justice system, and to prevent drunk driving crashes.

After their daughter Lisa was killed, Charlotte and Bob Hullinger founded Parents of Murdered Children as a support for other families forced to endure such tragedy.

The Compassionate Friends has over 600 groups around the country where parents of children who have died comfort each other. Rabbi Harold Kushner wrote *When Bad Things Happen to Good People* after his son died. He has continued to write other books which have been helpful to others.

Not all survivors will undertake such large and noble tasks in reaching out. But most are willing, even eager, to touch others who are surviving the loss of a loved one to a violent death. By doing so, they offer one of the most treasured gifts a human being can give to another.

## Suggestions

- Understand that the shock and injustice of losing someone you love to a sudden, violent, and senseless death can result in grief with a wider range and depth of feelings and grief which lasts longer than for survivors of anticipated, non-violent death. If you are coping well, wonderful! But if you are having a hard time, be patient with yourself. Many people struggle for months and years before they feel a resolution of their grieving.

- Maintain regular contact with your physician for several years to be sure that you do not acquire a stress-related physical condition.

- Try to delay major decisions for at least a year or more. Moving, remarrying, deciding to have a baby, changing jobs, no matter how positive they seem, will create additional stress.

- Feel your feelings—whether they be sadness, rage, vengeance, or others. Find a way to express them, perhaps through writing, perhaps by sharing them with someone else who understands, perhaps through physical activity. Try, though, to think rationally and to act responsibly.

- Take a realistic look at any guilt you feel. If you are guilty in part for what happened, try to forgive yourself (If God can, can't you?). Don't carry a load of guilt that isn't applicable to you.

- Try to be understanding of family members who may be grieving differently. It is rare for any two people in a family to handle trauma the same way. Remember that there are no rules for how one should grieve. Try to talk about what you are feeling, encourage others to do the same, and try to receive what you hear, even though your experience may be different.

- Be patient with others who say inept things to you. Very rarely are such comments made to hurt you. While most people desperately want to help you, they may not know what to say or do. Try to be grateful for their attempt, if not the end result.

- Remember that no one can fill the shoes of the loved one who has been killed. It is unrealistic to think that another person or activities can fill the vacuum now in your heart. Expecting another person to fulfill you places a terrible burden on him or her.

- Seek the support and understanding of others who have gone through the same kind of trauma. You and your family can benefit from the assistance of others. Call your local Mental Health Association, Hospice, and/or clergy to locate support groups and professional counselors who understand the grief that follows your kind of loss and trauma. You do not have to handle this alone.

- Realize that getting better does not mean that you didn't love your loved one enough. Nor does it mean that you will forget him or her. When and how you begin to feel better and what your pilgrimage toward recovery is like, are up to you.

# III

## DEATH OF A DAUGHTER OR SON

**M**other and Father as Parents

If you are a parent, you probably have spent much of your time thinking about how you would protect your children, nurture them into adulthood, and then "let go."

When parenting is successful, you expect your children to continue to love you as they become adults. You do not expect them to remain dependent on you. In fact, as you become older, you may depend on them to care for you. And in time, you expect to die and be survived by your children. When your child dies, every one of those expectations is aborted.

The way you nurture a child is different from the way you care for a mate, parents, or friends. When your child is very young, he is totally dependent on you. One amazing thing about human nature is that nurturing a baby, a toddler, or a young child is almost as fulfilling for the parent as it is for the child. That is true, however, only if the parent is emotionally healthy. Emotionally inadequate parents sometimes abuse or neglect their children.

If you are a healthy parent, you are so bonded to your young child that comforting him and keeping him content also makes you comfortable and content. The emptiness that remains when you no longer have your child to nurture can be so painful that some have referred to it as a chronic ache.

*This space is within me all the time it seems. Sometimes the empty space is so real I can almost touch it. I can almost see it. It gets so big sometimes I can't see anything else.*

Mary Sennewald[1]

As children grow older, they develop a sense of themselves that is separate from the parents. This separating from the parents prompts the new role of disciplining the child. This is a normal part of child development. Parents may feel an increasing need to protect their child as they see him or her grow up.

All children make mistakes. It is hard for a parent to decide when to step in and protect the child, and when to let the child learn by experiencing the consequences of his mistakes.

Parents are strongly driven, however, to protect their child from serious harm no matter how old their child is. Most parents say that if they had the choice, they would rather die themselves than to have their child seriously hurt or killed.

A difficult part of grieving for parents whose child has been killed is the fact that they were not able to protect their child. They may feel extremely angry at themselves for not preventing the tragedy. They may feel guilty, as if the child's death was their fault, even if they know it wasn't.

*All day long I listen for his step,*
*his whistle, his sweet, uncertain song.*
*I listen until the silence tightens*
*round my throat.*

*Oh God, you know I'd give my life*
*to hear his voice again.*

*To feel, once more, the touch of his*
*young, eager hand.*
*To stand and watch him play,*
*And feel the pride leap in me like a flame.*

*I'd give my life, I say—and yet*
*I wouldn't. I must stay here and*
*do my job until I've earned the right to go away.*

Elsie Robinson

Coping with the death of an older child is different from coping with the death of a young child. Parents may love them no more nor less, but their life experience with them is different. As children become older, they take more risks, check out more unknown territory, and try to solve their own problems. All of that is a very normal part of adolescent development. These phrases will probably have a familiar ring to parents of teenagers.

"I've got to be me!"

"You have got to let me grow up!"

"Get off my back. Weren't you ever a teenager?"

You may recall your child stomping out of the room or slamming doors. Parents are usually resistant to these kinds of words and behaviors. That, too, is normal. While the push and pull of raising a teenager is not always pleasant, it is a sign that the teen is looking for and finding his own values. That is good.

When an older child is killed, parents may have a very difficult time realizing that they were doing the right thing by allowing their child to take risks. If you chose to allow your child some freedom, and it resulted in your child's death, it will not help to place all the blame on yourself. You probably made the best decision you knew how to make at the time.

*So many recollections bring you to me-*
*Your insistence on being just you-*
*"Stubborn," we said.*
*But no, you were "right.."*
*You knew what you wanted since age two.*

*Friends, problems, college life, romance from afar,*
*Sorority joys, world troubles, future dreams*
*"Mom, don't expect grandkids or even marriage for*
*  awhile...*
*....maybe never."*

*You prepared me it seems.*

*Thank you, Valerie, for being our daughter.*
*Your mother and dad love you so.*
*We didn't tell you that very often.*
*So now our tears must let you know.*

Katherine D. Guayante,
in memory of Valerie.

Another component of grieving, if your child has been killed, has to do with your investment which has now come to naught. You invested heavily in your child emotionally. Even if you faced difficult days with your child, you developed dreams for his future. As your child grew older, you noted special talents and interests. Your child may have spent time talking with you about what she wanted to be or do upon growing up.

You probably invested financially in those dreams. You purchased insurance policies to ensure that your child would have enough money when you die. You may have paid for braces, for music lessons. You may have encouraged your child to develop skills in sports or other physical activities. You may have bought calculators or computers to help your child achieve. You may have borrowed money or set aside funds to help your child through college.

Parents would gladly pay it all again, and a thousand times over, if they could have their child back. But that isn't possible. It may help, however, to understand that your financial investment was symbolic of your emotional investment. It may help you understand why a child's death seems so deeply wrong.

Having a child killed is not only to lose someone you feel driven to nurture and protect, but it is also to lose hopes and dreams for the future.

*No words can ever describe the pain of losing a child. On that night in April, 1984, a large part of my inner self died along with my only daughter. All of her hopes and dreams are gone. She will never graduate from high school, go to college, or experience the special love of a husband and children. All those things she spoke of so often are gone, and with them so much of my future. The void will be with me for the rest of my life.*

> Ginger Babb, writing about her 17 year-old daughter, Julie, who was killed.

## Mother and Father as Mates

The killing of a child can have a tremendous impact on the marriage of the parents. Some couples find that the tragedy draws them closer together. This can happen when they communicate openly and support each other as first one, and then the other, has bad days. It is not uncommon, however, for the marital relationship to break down in the aftermath of a tragedy so great as the killing of their child.

It is very difficult to support and nurture your mate when your own grief is overwhelming. When experiencing trauma, most people regress to a childlike state. They feel vulnerable and need to be "taken care of." If both mates are in the same condition, and neither has the strength to care for the other, feelings of alienation will emerge.

41

*This morning, upon my husband's pillow,*
*A tear.*
*Last night I heard no weeping,*
*I felt no rhythmic shaking.*
*Yet there it is,*
*Glistening, silent testimony to pain.*

*Quickly I reached to blot it*
*As if one swift brush*
*Could set the world right again.*
*But something stops my hand,*
*Stops me to wonder:*
*Am I the cause of weeping?*

*In my life is much sorrow,*
*Dreadful longing and much emptiness*
*That even my husband cannot fill.*
*Sorrow brings sleepless nights in fear*
*Of other phone calls and ambulances;*
*More longing and emptiness.*
*My husband shares this loss*
*But men don't cry.*
*They nod gravely and tend to details,*
*Make arrangements and give support.*
*Yet, there it is upon his pillow:*
*A tear.*

*Have I given way to grief*
*And forgotten one who shares?*
*Have I made no room for his tears*
*In the flood of mine?*
*Am I the reason he weeps*
*Only in the silence of the night?*

*I close my hand*
*To leave the tear drying there.*
*No more will I blot out his pain*
*To tend to mine,*
*For we must share*
*In order to live—together.*

Marcia Alig


Because your drive to nurture and protect has been violently interrupted, you will probably have a strong need to assess blame. As previously discussed, many parents blame themselves and feel guilty. It is also tempting to blame your mate.

If a child has a terminal illness, it is usually no one's fault. Parents can become very angry that science has not found a cure or the treatment was not successful. But, when they are able to care for their child as he is dying, they can know that they did everything they could.

When a child is killed, someone was at fault. If the cause of the killing is not explicitly clear, parents may engage in a relentless search for the causes. They can usually find a way to blame the other parent, at least in part.

Blaming will intensify the impact of the trauma. It can be a major factor in the breakup of marriage following the death of a child. It may also lead to the premature death of some parents within three to five years after the death of their child.

Another component of stress between mates is the fact that rarely do two people move through grieving in the same way.

As a father, you may choose to grieve privately. You may be angry, deeply resenting the loss of control you feel when you think about your child's death.

As a mother, you may be more open with your grief. You want to talk about it, to cry with someone who understands. You may be more sorrowful and wonder how your mate has the energy to be so angry. On another day, these roles may be reversed.

One of you may cry at the mention or even the thought of the child who has been killed, while the other may function well enough to return to work. One may read books to better understand what is happening while the other refuses to face it. One may want to go to a support group of fellow sufferers while the other feels repulsed at the mention of it. It is very difficult to understand and accept each other's grieving when they are so different.

*I felt different emotions than my husband did. I felt compassion for the other driver, feeling his conscience would punish him. My husband wanted him to pay dearly. Then there was, for a time, so much guilt—if Mike had a bigger, faster car, a daytime job-so many "ifs." My husband seemed to have a larger problem with this than I did. I only wished I had said "I love you" more often.*

Rita Chiavacci

A very practical side of these differences is seen when it comes to deciding what to do with the child's "things." One may be eager to dismantle the child's room and discard clothing and mementos. The other may believe that to do so would deny the existence of the child. Trying to find a happy medium for these polarities may be difficult.

Many couples are distressed to learn that jealousy and envy rear their ugly heads during grieving.

If you are depressed and apathetic, and are at home, you may envy your mate who is at work because you fantasize that he or she can be happy there with the many distractions that a job entails. If you are the one working, you may envy the mate at home who can face the grief and not have to "hold up to get the job done."

A father may envy the mother who says she feels a closeness to the child that the father can't because she carried the child in her body for nine months and birthed it.

Mates may have unrealistic expectations of each other regarding work load and maintenance of the home. Sloppy housekeeping or failure to mow the lawn may infuriate a mate who is depending on the other to stay on top of things. Many couples say it takes months before they have enough energy to do more than what simply has to be done.

Sexuality can become a divisive issue during bereavement. Your mate may face an increased need for sex as nurture, escape, or release, while you are repulsed at the thought of it. Avoidance of sex can stem from fear of having and losing other children. It can be rooted in guilt over experiencing pleasure when something so awful has happened. Or it can manifest as a classic symptom of depression.

If your barriers to feelings are let down in order to experience the closeness of sexual intimacy, then the flood gate is also opened to pain and grief. Since sexual intimacy and orgasm can put you in touch with feelings at a deep level, you may avoid it for fear of tapping into uncontrollably painful emotional release. This can be complicated by the fact that your mate may have mannerisms or physical attributes similar to that of the dead child. To be reminded so potently of the child's death when approaching sexual intimacy can be devastating.

Any of these problems can cause you or your mate to back away from sexual contact. Then the avoidance, if not talked about, can be perceived as additional rejection. For example, your mate may perceive you as unresponsive and totally wrapped up in your grief when you say you are not interested in sex. Your mate may then perceive you as insensitive. In fact, both of you are hurting and are trying to minimize your own unique pain.

Unfortunately, your mate is the easiest target for venting all types of frustrations. You spend many hours together. Your defenses are down more at home than anywhere else. It is important for you to understand that these problems nearly always arise. You will be fortunate if they don't.

But if they do, try to understand that they are normal consequences of having your child killed suddenly and violently. You don't feel normal. But you are normal in the sense that pain and struggle following major surgery are normal. A very significant part of your life has been cut out. The process of getting better requires time and patience and hard work.

An oft-quoted myth is that 80% to 90% of marriages fail when a child dies. Studies reaching this conclusion failed to take normal divorce rates into account and were based on couples already in marital counseling. We now know that when divorce does follow the death of a child, it is usually the result of problems that existed before the death. Perhaps the marital problems no longer seemed reconcilable after the death of the child. Some of the positive aspects of living through trauma—reordered priorities, a sense of endurance, and new-found assertiveness—may contribute to the decision to go ahead and divorce. But, in fact, most marriages **do** survive the death of a child.

## How Long Will It Take?

You are no longer the same person you were before your child was killed. To expect that you will ever be exactly the same is to place an unrealistic burden on yourself.

It is also impossible to place a timetable on your grieving. Remember that many factors play into it and, therefore, you will develop your own timetable.

Some begin to feel better as they are able to make sense of what happened by learning all the facts. Some begin to feel better after the court case is disposed of.

Many people say that the second year is harder than the first. Most people feel noticeably better by the third or fourth year, although some say the third year is harder than the second.

46

Research shows that most survivors feel significantly better by the fourth year.

There will always be good days and bad days. But the pain will decrease as time goes on. You will one day be surprised to learn that you can feel sad without becoming engulfed in grief. You will find it possible to be happy, if only for a short period of time. Having friends and family who love you and accept you as you are is a blessing. They may be more important than anyone else in helping you get better.

You may want to keep a journal or diary. They are a good way to see your progress. You may be surprised to learn that what you wrote today shows marked improvement over what you wrote three months ago. It is hard to say when healing starts, but when looking back, it is easier to see.

## Suggestions

- Remember that your family is not a "bad family" or your marriage a "bad marriage" because difficult problems arise. It would be unusual if they did not because recovery from the death of a child is one of the most difficult tasks any family can undertake.

- Try to understand that it is rare for any two people to grieve the same way. Pay attention to your own grieving needs and do what feels right for you. Likewise, try to respect the needs of others who live in your household.

- Try to keep talking with your mate and with surviving children about how you feel. Attempting to hide your feelings from your family is like covering a cancer with a bandaid. The pain always comes through. You will all be healthier if the pain is out in the open. It is good for you to cry together.

- If your family is unable or unwilling to support you in your grieving, look for a support group of people who understand. Consider the organizations that have been formed to help grieving parents, such as Mothers Against

Drunk Driving, Parents of Murdered Children, Victims for Victims and Compassionate Friends. Look for a counselor, chaplain, minister, or rabbi with skills in helping people who are experiencing grief following trauma.

- Collect as much information as possible about how your child was killed. This information can be obtained from police reports, from autopsy reports, and by talking to witnesses. It is important to collect this data for two reasons: your mind will rest better if you can "make sense" of the experience; and, through collecting data, blame and responsibility can be placed appropriately.

- When disagreements and misunderstandings occur in your family, try not to vent anger by yelling, or screaming, or verbally attacking. Own your anger, but try not to target someone else in your family. Say "I love you" every time you feel even a hint of love. These words will be cherished.

- If sexual needs differ between you and your mate, talk about it and try to reach a reasonable compromise. Hugs and tenderly holding each other can be lifesavers, even when more explicit sexuality may not be possible.

- Consider keeping a journal or a diary. It can be helpful not only in giving you a way to release your feelings, but also in helping you measure your recovery.

- Remember that allowing yourself to feel better does not mean that you are forgetting or being disloyal to your child. It means continuing to grieve but becoming less overwhelmed by it. It means that you believe that life, as it goes on, matters. For your own sake and for others who need and love you, you have a responsibility to try to feel better.

- Have patience. Realize that the traditional "one year of grief" is not enough. Only a combination of time and hard work will lead to resolution of the pain and you will never be totally free of it. How hard you work at it and how long it takes are up to you.

1. Reprinted courtesy of St. Louis Information and Counseling Program for Sudden Infant Death.

# IV

# DEATH OF BROTHER OR SISTER

*Special Bond.*
*Precious Relationship.*
*Profound Loss.*
*Sister. Brother.*
*Painful void.*
*Please Understand.*

Jean Lewis

The death of a brother or sister is a crisis for children and it is a crisis for adult siblings. Yet, they are often neglected grievers because so much focus is placed on the parents of a small child or the remaining spouse and children of an adult sibling. Young siblings are vulnerable to emotional problems following trauma. Interestingly, though, many children seem to cope with it better than adults.

Much of what we understand about adult grieving is also true for children:

- A sudden violent death requires different coping skills than an anticipated non-violent death.

- If a child has emotional difficulties before the death of a sibling, and/or if the family suffers marital discord, the child may be more vulnerable to long-term effects of the trauma.

- If a child's brother or sister is killed at a time when their relationship was troubled, as in sibling rivalry, the death may be more difficult to handle.

- If a child has emotional support from the parent(s) or major caretaker following the death, and expression of feelings is encouraged, the child will probably adjust satisfactorily.

If you are a parent whose child has been killed, you may be needed by too many people. You may find yourself comforting your mate, relatives, or friends because they can't come to grips with what has happened to your family. At some point, their needs can overwhelm you, and you must withdraw to survive.

As you observe your surviving children experiencing the trauma, you may be tempted to put them on a plane or bus and send them off to be with someone else who loves them. You wish you could help them escape the pain—and you feel guilty because you can't comfort them. Simply "hanging on" yourself may be your top priority or the only task you can handle.

It is best for families to grieve together. A young child should not witness the total collapse of a parent, but tears which overflow out of sadness for what has happened are to be shared.

It is impossible to go through life without hurting. It would be wonderful if we could promise our children life without pain. We can't. Grieving together will teach your child that ugly and unfair things happen, and that all of you can survive them.

Young children don't just look to their parents as models. They usually believe, at least until they reach adolescence, that parents are all-powerful and all-knowing. They will trust you more than ever if you are honest about your feelings and if you do not tell them half-truths about the killing of your child. A child who watches a lot of television or sees a lot of movies may have warped ideas about death. Therefore, honest communication can result in valuable lessons for your child.

Like adults, children differ in the way they react to death. Their age, their ethnic customs, their religious beliefs, the relationship they had with the brother or sister who was killed, will all make a difference. The most important component is how you, the parent, relate to them in the aftermath of the killing.

Children are not miniature adults. Children have their own distinct way of understanding things. Much of that is determined by how old they are.

Young children differ from adults in that they can endure strong feelings for only a short period of time. As an adult, you may feel that your grief goes on and on. A few years from now you will look back and see that you are better than you were before, but now it may seem that the pain is constant.

A child, on the other hand, grieves deeply for awhile and then seems to be content and carefree. Maybe tomorrow, he will misbehave or show a violent outburst of anger, while later that evening he will want to play games.

Children grieve on an intermittent basis for years after the death of their brother or sister. As they move through their developmental stages, they will understand death in a new way and grieve all over again according to their new understanding or level of emotional maturity. Developmental levels vary greatly in children, as do their environments. Therefore, a child's specific age is not always a clear indicator of how she will grieve. The age ranges below should be interpreted very liberally.

**Infants And Toddlers**

Before the age of three months or so, a baby may be as content with other caretakers as he is with his mother, unless the mother is nursing. He has little, if any, memory of family members when they are out of sight. If a constant caretaker continues to nurture and care for him, he will have minimal reaction to a loss in the family.

As the infant grows, he usually develops anxiety when around strangers—a sign that he has bonded to his mother or major caretaker. From that age on, a child who loses a parent will grieve. He clearly knows the parent and depends on the parent to feed him, clothe and bathe him, talk to him, and play with him. His grieving the loss of a parent may look like a diffused sense of distress with whimpering, loss of appetite, loss of speech if he has learned to talk, and finally, quiet resignation. A toddler is not likely, however, to deeply grieve the loss of a brother or sister unless the sibling has assumed a major caretaking role.

A toddler will pick up on the feelings expressed in the home. That is why calm nurturing is important. Explanations about death won't have meaning for him. What the people who love him do is more important than what they say. Holding, cuddling, and stroking are ways of assuring him that he is cared for. They are more important than words.

## Ages Four Through Six

A child in this age range is still unable to understand what death is or that it is permanent. It is likely, though, that he or she has discovered dead birds in the yard or has seen something dead which was simply picked up and discarded. A young child may respond to the death of a sibling, therefore, in a rather matter of fact manner. He may speak of the death of his sibling almost as he would the death of a pet. He may be aware that something bad has happened, but not that it is devastating. This can be terribly upsetting to parents who don't understand that for his level of understanding, he is responding normally.

The death of a brother or sister is best explained to a young child in physical terms because his thinking is very concrete. "Your brother was in his car when another car crashed into it. It hit so hard that his body got crushed inside the car. It was broken so badly that his heart stopped working and no one could get it to start up again. So, your brother doesn't breathe anymore. He can't talk or move anymore. He doesn't have feelings. He can't feel hot or cold, or wet or dry. He can't feel happy or sad. His body doesn't feel anything anymore, so we will bury his body in the ground (or whatever your family's choice is for the final resting place of the body)."

A child this age will have difficulty understanding the concept of soul or spirit. If you believe in a spiritual afterlife, it is still important to explain to your child that his brother's or sister's body will be buried or cremated. You might explain that the part that now lives in Heaven is the part that was able to love and have feelings.

If your child is told that his brother or sister has "gone to Heaven and is now happy with God," but the family is extremely upset, and the child later learns that his sibling is at the funeral home or the cemetery, he will not only be confused, but he will feel betrayed.

Your child aged four through six has a sense of right and wrong, not so much because of an inner sense of morality, but because he has been praised for doing "good" things and punished for doing "bad" things. He still clings to many mystical beliefs based on fairy tales he hears and television shows he watches. Therefore, it is quite easy for him to believe that his brother or sister was killed because he did something bad. If he has wished his sibling would go away—as all brothers and sisters sometimes do—he may be convinced his wishing made it so. Most children have death wishes. Your family has been invaded by death. Your child may assume, therefore, that it's his fault.

It is extremely important for your child to know that the death of his brother or sister was not his fault. Explaining death in concrete, physical terms will be helpful to him.

Because your young child is still limited in his vocabulary, especially when it comes to describing feelings, he is likely to try to master his loss through play. You can be very supportive to your child if you pay attention to his play, whether it be re-enacting the killing, playing funeral, or playing "house." Asking questions such as, "Why is the little brother crying?" can help your child begin to verbalize what he feels.

It would not be unusual for your child at this age to develop eating or sleeping problems. As a matter of fact, you can almost expect sleeping problems if your child has heard that his brother or sister "died in their sleep" or that dying is "just like going to sleep."

Bowel or bladder control problems can also return and are fairly common symptoms of emotional stress. If the problems are intense or last so long that you feel they are interfering with your child's health, a doctor should be consulted.

## Ages Seven through Eleven

Somewhere in this age range, your child will come to the understanding that death is final and that everyone eventually dies. This awareness can be traumatic for the child because he is still so dependent on his family that he can't imagine surviving without them. He may realize that he, too, will die. This new awareness is frightening for any child. But when his brother or sister, who is likely near his own age, has been killed, he must face death intimately. He also now realizes that it is not just old people who die.

*My big brother Joshua Erik Jones—9 years old got hit by a car July 8th, 1985. I feel very VERY SAD. <u>I am very VERY MAD at the man who killed my brother!</u> He was really very very drunk. He does not have to stay in jail very long. And I am mad about that too. That man was very very bad! I hope Josh is learning a lot up with God. I don't like to sleep in my bed with out Josh in the bedroom. I miss Josh very very much. I loved Josh very very much.*

The End

Jessica Jones, Age 7

For children this age, death is seen as an attacker who intrudes and takes life. Your child may be very fearful that he, too, will be killed. It is a realistic fear, based on what has happened. It would not be unusual for your child to develop fears or phobias about anything related to death. He may complain of physical ailments, withdraw, and become excessively careful and cautious. Children in this age range are more likely than other children to exhibit behavior problems following the death of a sibling. This may especially be true if they are the only remaining child in the family.

If your child is in this age range, he has had more years to experience sibling rivalry, more memories of fights with his brother or sister, and more death wishes.

Even more than when he was younger, he may feel that he was responsible for the killing of his brother or sister. He is not intellectually mature enough to persuade himself of his innocence, so he will need help in correctly assessing blame. As you will recall from previous chapters, parents also struggle with tremendous guilt when a child in the family has been killed.

The child in this age range now has an expansive vocabulary and can think abstractly enough to openly express his pain, fears, anger, and guilt. He is not only sensitive to his own feelings, but he can also enter into the feelings of others. He is able to empathize. He not only needs comfort and support, but he can be a source of comfort and support to others. Doing so will make him feel better. He must never be led to believe, though, that he is responsible for making the family feel better. He is not a parent. He is still a child.

It is important that your child participate fully in the family's grieving. He should be told the truth. If he has never attended a funeral before, he should be told ahead of time exactly what to expect. He should share in decisions about the funeral and in grieving rituals during the months and years following. He should be encouraged to be open in his grieving. And you should not hide your grieving from him.

A word of caution is called for regarding this age range. Because your child can comprehend something of the depths of your despair, he may attempt to, in some way, replace his brother or sister who has been killed as a means of helping you cope. You must tell him clearly that no one can replace your child who has been killed. You must help your surviving child to understand that the place in your heart for him, likewise, can be filled by no other.

Another word of caution has to do with putting the child who was killed on a pedestal. It is important for you to remember your child who was killed as realistically as possible. Because of guilt concerning the bad times, it is easy to push those times out of consciousness and recall your child as nearly perfect. This can be devastating for siblings. To them, it appears that you love them less and that they can never measure up to what they witness you expressing about your dead child. This can cause them to withdraw now, or later when they reach adolescence.

A child in this age range may have difficulty in school. Grieving children are confused and have difficulty concentrating, much like their parents. If the school problems continue after months, they may be a sign of deeper underlying stress which may need professional attention.

## Adolescent Siblings

The developmental goal of adolescence is to "leave home"—to begin to leave emotionally, and eventually to leave physically. In the process of preparing to separate, your child becomes less family oriented and more peer oriented. He finds out who he is and what he believes by venturing out into unknown territory.

He is basically insecure and may be somewhat self-centered in order to compensate. He is suffering a lot of losses as he moves through adolescence—the loss of security of having mother and father make decisions for him, the loss of innocence, and the loss of protection by his family.

Because your adolescent is shaky and insecure, the sudden death of a brother or sister is something he definitely does not want to face. He knows he must, but he may frantically try to escape it. He faces several dilemmas. He is mature enough to understand life like an adult. On the other hand, he is more vulnerable than adults because he is experiencing so many other losses and changes.

A teenager has the capacity for empathy, but because he is basically self-centered—as he has to be in order to become "his own person"—he may feel that no one has ever felt the deep and powerful things that he is now experiencing. Indeed, most adolescents have not experienced anything as devastating as the killing of a brother or sister. While a teen needs to lean on his parents for support, he may be reluctant to let these deep emotions show because he is afraid he will seem child-like again.

*Our three boys were hit by a drunk driver—Dennis and Tim were killed instantly. Jeff survived. It's been six months, and our sixteen year-old daughter, Pam, still cannot talk about the boys. My husband and Jeff rarely do.*

Ilene Hammon

The adolescent may be coping with the same struggles as the younger child—guilt over sibling rivalry, especially if he recently had open conflict with the brother or sister who was killed. He may feel he should take care of parents who are devastated, or even try to take the place of the dead sibling. As a bereaved parent you may be inclined to turn to your surviving adolescent child for emotional support. Such an expectation, if constant, can be overwhelming. It can also impede your adolescent's "growing up," pulling away from family and becoming more intimate with peers.

An additional source of stress for the surviving adolescent sibling is over-protectiveness on the part of the parent. It is almost impossible for a parent whose child has been killed not to have great anxiety when another adolescent is out with friends on his own. Such over-protectiveness feels stifling and smothering to the adolescent.

All of these pressures coming together for the surviving adolescent can cause him to become self-destructive and engage in alcohol or other drug abuse, running away from home, or taking risks such as playing "chicken" in an automobile. Flirting with death, so to speak, can be a way of trying to gain control of it. It can also be an escape. Moving fast, keeping the music loud, and forfeiting reality by using drugs are choices he can make to escape the pain.

As parents of an adolescent who has lost a brother or sister, try to be honest and provide emotional support, but don't be surprised if he needs to escape. Doing so, to some degree, is part of normal adolescent development. It becomes even more understandable when the home is filled with so much pain and he is frightened by his own feelings.

Your adolescent may talk more to his friends about his brother's or sister's death than he does to you. He may respond better to another adult who is willing to listen because he does not have to worry about his pain hurting that person as much as it hurts you. You should not be discouraged if he reaches out to someone other than you. That is normal for his stage of development.

## Adult Siblings

Most people misunderstand how deeply adult siblings grieve. If your sibling was older than you, you have shared life with him or her as long as you have had your parents. Even if your sibling was younger, you may not remember life without him or her.

A sibling relationship carries with it a bond that preference cannot sever. When your sibling was killed you not only lost a unique loved one, but you lost that person's role within the family as well. If your sibling was the person who organized the family parties, either someone else must now take on that role or your family will be acutely aware of the absence. If your brother was the peacemaker during family quarrels, someone else must now take on that responsibility. It is normal that you and other siblings will try to "fill in" some of these roles. Some changes may take place quite naturally and easily while others may feel awkward and cause a great deal of conflict within the family.

Part of your role within the family may be related to birth order. If your oldest sibling was killed, you may have lost a caregiver or someone to whom you've always looked up. If the "baby" of the family was killed, you may have lost the one you protected the most. If the age difference was great enough between you and the brother or sister who was killed, you may feel almost as though you have lost a parent or a child.

When a brother or sister dies, you also experience a gap in birth order. If the oldest sibling was killed, the second oldest is now the oldest. If there were just two of you, you are now an only child.

If the sibling killed was your twin or part of a multiple birth, you probably feel that part of yourself died too. You will need to work hard at rational thinking to prevent you from concluding that the wrong one died.

Many bereaved siblings find it difficult to answer social questions. When someone casually asks, "How many brothers and sisters do you have?" or, "How many are there in your family?" you may feel unable to respond. There is no "right" way to answer these questions and you may answer differently from time to time depending on how you feel and the setting in which you find yourself.

Assuming you had three brothers and one was killed, you may want to say, "I have three brothers; two are living, one was killed." You may want to say, "I have three brothers," and leave it at that. Or, you may want to say, "I have two brothers." You have the right to answer these questions in any way you feel comfortable.

For some bereaved siblings, the fact that their sibling's death has altered their relationship with their parents is deeply painful. Chances are, under the stress of coping with the death of their child, your parents will react to you in some ways as though you were still a small child. They are struggling with the senselessness and the unnaturalness of being predeceased by one of their children.

You may find your parents are trying to comfort you at the expense of themselves, or are trying to protect you from the reality of death. They may be terrified that another family member may be killed and go to great lengths to monitor your activities. If this behavior is creating a barrier within the family, you may need to talk with your parents and offer them some concrete ways that they can be supportive of you. In turn, invite them to tell you what you could do to comfort them the most. In times of crisis it is very easy to fall into old parent/child habits, but it doesn't have to be that way. They will need to give a little —but so will you.

Similarly, you may find yourself falling into old patterns of behavior in an effort to protect your parents. You may feel they hurt enough without having to watch you grieve. You may go to incredible lengths to hide your pain from them. It may seem right for you to make decisions for your parents or take on parental responsibilities in an effort to care for them. You may end up "parenting your parents." Usually, though, adult children and parents care for one another because it gives them something to do with their grief. Ask if your parents feel you are over-protecting or smothering them. Respect their response and accommodate as best you can.

In some ways you may feel as though, in addition to the loss of your sibling, you've lost your parents. Your parents may always have been strong and there for you in times of crisis. Even if you aren't very close to your parents, it can be incredibly painful to become aware of their vulnerability and weakness. This may be the first time you've turned to your parents for support and they can't solve the problem and make it better for you. You may need to grieve the loss of your parents - the parents that were always strong, always in control, never vulnerable.

Ultimately, you will likely forge a new relationship with your parents. Talk with them about what you observe and ask them to share with you how they see you differently. Tell them you want to use these new understandings to build a new, more mature, relationship with them.

Like watching a rock tossed into the lake, you may experience other losses connected with your sibling's death. If your brother or sister married, your family may lose contact with the husband or wife and with the children, if there were any. If you want to stay close with them, you may have to be direct about your desires and take the responsibility for staying in touch. Eventually most widows and widowers remarry, which can be extremely painful to the family of the dead husband or wife. Remember, if you can, that no one will replace your brother or sister and remarrying isn't an act of disloyalty. A new spouse will probably be very uncertain about his or her relationship with your family, and will welcome some clarification from you.

If your sibling had children, they will likely be precious reminders of your brother and sister. Discovering traits and physical features in nieces and nephews that are similar to those of your brother or sister is both joyous and painful. Similarly, the special moments in their lives—graduations, marriages, the births of their children—will be bittersweet as they will always highlight your sibling's absence from these events. Children, especially those who were small when their parent was killed, will want to learn about that parent from you and others. Maintaining a relationship with nieces and nephews is one way some bereaved siblings have found to honor the memory of their brother or sister.

If you are married, your own spouse may feel like one of the forgotten victims. Your spouse may have had a very special relationship with your sister or brother yet doesn't have the same official ties with your family. Don't forget to include your

61

spouse and the spouses of other brothers and sisters in family events following the death of your sibling. They have also lost the person you were before your brother or sister was killed. While their grief may be different, it needs to be recognized and accepted just as is yours.

## Suggestions

- Be careful about explaining death in half-truths to younger children who need honest, concrete explanations of what has happened. If the child hears, "Your sister has gone away for a very long time," he may feel that his sister has deserted him. He may then go on to interpret the desertion as punishment and have strong feelings of guilt. "Your brother has gone to heaven," is in itself impossible for a young child to understand, especially when he learns that the body is buried in the cemetery. "To die is to go to sleep," can be understood by the child as a very real reason for refusing to go to sleep. "Your sister went to the hospital and died," can cause a young child to conclude that hospitals make people die. "Your brother died because he got sick," may cause a child to become extremely fearful of any kind of illness.

- Spend time in play with the younger child who may not have adequate communication skills to talk about his feelings.

- Help your child express his feelings by being willing to express yours, and asking your child questions. If he is reluctant, phrase questions as if they were someone else's, "What would you say to Jimmy if he asked you what happened to your brother?"

- Remember that most children grieve intermittently rather than chronically. Therefore, do not be upset because your child has periods when the death of his brother or sister seems unimportant.

- Children may find it easier than parents to discard personal possessions of the deceased. They may also find it easier to "put their grief aside" and find normalcy in school or play. Remember that your deceased child's friends may be pleased to be given something that belonged to your child.

- Protect young children from witnessing an emotional collapse, but otherwise share as much of the grieving as possible.

- During the early days of grieving, it is helpful for grieving children to have a personal "ally" to provide stability and understanding. This person calms the anxious child and relieves the parents of total responsibility.

- Siblings aged six or seven or older should be given all the facts about their brother's or sister's death as they become known. Not being told the truth only enhances a growing sense of being unimportant in the family.

- If you see another child who reminds you of your child who has been killed, point this out to the siblings and explain the grief spasm it has caused. Mysterious behavior on the part of the parent only enhances the sibling's fear of being left out or of not being loved as much as the deceased child.

- Share your grief with your surviving children, but do not depend on them to take care of you in your grieving. Understand that adolescent children may not want to grieve with you.

- Talk with surviving brothers and sisters both about pleasant memories of the child who was killed as well as unpleasant memories. This will help them to understand that the child who died was not perfect. Placing the dead child on a pedestal can cause great insecurity for surviving siblings.

- Don't ask surviving siblings to "be strong" for you or for anyone else. That is too great a burden to carry.

- Try not to feel threatened if adolescent siblings seek out other adults or peers for support. That is normal for their developmental level.

- As an adult sibling, spend some time focusing on the role of your brother and sister in the family and how you can enable a meaningful transition to the family which now is. Be gentle with yourself and with your parents.

# NOTES

# V

## DEATH OF A MATE OR LOVER

The killing of a husband, wife or lover is among the most stressful of losses. No matter what your age, you are not ready to be suddenly abandoned by the person you depended on the most.

Many books are on the market which address the death of a spouse, so in this chapter we will focus primarily on aspects which relate to sudden death.

### Roles and Responsibilities

Your mate probably fulfilled many roles in your household and in your life. Your mate was co-manager of your home and co-parent of your children. Together you decided how to spend money, what kind of jobs to have, how to discipline children, and where and when to entertain yourselves. Your mate may have been your best friend.

If you and your mate shared most of these roles, you may now feel overwhelmed with assuming all of them yourself.

In some relationships, couples choose to separate responsibilities rather than share them. For example, one partner may pay all the bills, maintain the car and yard, decide on major purchases, and do the financial record keeping for the family. The other may be responsible for in-home maintenance, child care and for planning entertainment. The sudden loss of one of the partners, in this kind of relationship, can cause feelings of helplessness and vulnerability that make coping extremely difficult. The surviving partner must suddenly assume new roles which seem awkward and frustrating. To be forced to learn a number of new roles in the midst of grieving is a monumental task.

You may never have operated a clothes washer or dryer. You may never have planned a weekly menu and shopping list. You may not know how to cook. You may be totally ignorant about automobile maintenance. You may not know how to make repairs around the house. You may have no idea what kind of records should be kept for income tax purposes. You may not understand about certain bank accounts, annuities, investments or other financial matters for which you are now responsible.

Frustrations such as these are exaggerated if you, as the surviving partner, also now have sole responsibility for children, each of whom, like you, feels abandoned and is grieving in his or her own way.

In addition to all of this, the issue of income rears its ugly head. If your mate who was killed provided all or part of the household income, you may face a complete change in living style. See Chapter XI of this book for suggestions in coping with financial matters. These will help you through the first months. But, in terms of long range planning, you may eventually need to make major changes in order to be responsible and survive financially.

You can expect changes in the way you are perceived by your friends. If you and your mate shared social relationships with other couples, you may find that you no longer "fit" in the group. Being with them can make you feel terribly alone. You may now feel uncomfortable relating to other people's mates for fear they might become jealous if they sense you are potential competition. If many of your social relationships were centered around your mate's employment or circle of friends, you may no longer feel you belong.

Finally, one of the most difficult aspects of the death of a mate is the absence of physical intimacy. Sexual interest may wane as you grieve, but most people continue to need touching and holding. These yearnings will probably go unsatisfied until another relationship can be established. Your interest in a new relationship may be the last thing on your mind for some time. But this can change depending on your age and the quality of the previous relationship.

## Dependence/Independence

To enhance the healing process, it is important to understand dependency/independence issues as you try to endure the death of your mate. It is usual for two people living together to be emotionally dependent on each other. The degree of dependence you placed on your mate may have a lot to do with how quickly you feel better.

Some couples are so dependent that each one feels only half of a whole. With the other half gone, they have difficulty imagining that they could ever function alone.

**BEFORE**         **NOW**

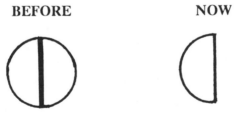

Some couples share responsibilities but experience themselves as two independent individuals who rarely "need" each other to feel good about themselves.

**BEFORE**          **NOW**

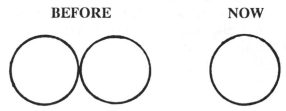

Other couples feel primarily independent but realize that each has various aspects of life in which one depends on the other. They experience both dependence and independence.

**BEFORE**          **NOW**

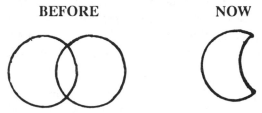

Mates with some degree of independence will probably cope with the death better than those who are excessively dependent. If you were in a very emotionally dependent relationship, you will have the task, eventually of learning how to be a more independent person, give up your image as a "partnerless half," and enhance your sense of individuality.

If you successfully moved away from your parents and achieved a sense of independence and autonomy before entering a relationship with a mate or partner, this process may be one of re-discovery. On the other hand, if you were originally dependent on your parents and then become immediately dependent on your mate, the process may be new for you.

Re-discovering your own autonomy may require dramatic growth if you decide to work on it at the same time you are grieving the death of your mate. You may find a grief therapist or marital counselor helpful if you feel you are getting stuck. Or you might choose to work in a more slow, quiet way, testing your independence daily until you see that you have re-oriented and adjusted.

While such growth and adjustment toward autonomy is tedious and painful, most surviving spouses who have experienced it believe that it is worth the effort. They learn that they can endure independently. Spouses also feel a sense of satisfaction that they can eventually form another relationship because of desire, not need.

How does this kind of growth manifest itself? It can mean moving from indecisiveness to feeling good about independent decision-making. It can mean shifting from helplessness to helpfulness. It can mean replacing intense yearning with sorrow for what you no longer have coupled with a celebration of what you had, which continues to be yours.

Your situation might be different. Perhaps you were the more independent mate and your partner who was killed was dependent on you. You don't feel helpless and indecisive, but you wonder why you feel so anxious and lonely. Some people "need to be needed." Parents nearly always feel some degree of this when their children are small, but they outgrow it as their children need them less and less. Perhaps you chose to live with a partner who needed you. If so, you now may feel unimportant.

In order to feel better, you may look for other relationships with dependent people. If you send out conscious or unconscious signals that you like dependent people, you surely will find them.

Perhaps you will want to re-evaluate the pros and cons of an independent-dependent relationship. You may want to consider what it was like for your mate to have been so dependent on you. You may decide that you want future relationships to be different.

## Satisfying/Difficult Relationships

All people have some ambivalence in their relationships. In the most affectionate of relationships, couples experience instances of anger, even hostility. However, most relationships are either basically satisfying or basically conflict-ridden.

If your relationship with your mate was generally satisfying, if it was mutually rewarding, and if you have few guilt-producing memories, you will probably cope better than others whose relationships were conflict-ridden.

Consider the loss of a satisfying relationship. Looking closely, you may find that although you deeply grieve the death of your mate, you have little about which to feel remorseful or guilty. You have many memories to cherish. You can say that your life together was something to be celebrated.

If your relationship with your mate was often conflict-ridden, you may experience some sense of relief from the conflict as the shock of the death wears off, but it may be replaced with a remorse you don't understand. Even though the relationship was negative, the feelings and attachment may have been strong. A difficult relationship is still a relationship.

You may feel guilty because you weren't better able to work things out. You may be obsessed with memories you wish you could forget. Even though you know it's impossible, you long for another chance to make your relationship different. Sometimes the guilt is so painful, that you unconsciously repress it and actually forget the hostility you previously felt. What you feel becomes, literally, too much to bear.

This is not unlike what children from unhappy homes experience when they are moved out of their family into a foster home. They soon forget about the abuse and may long to return home. They are convinced that any problems in the family were their own fault and they are sure it would be different, if they could only be reunited with their families.

Wishing for another chance when you know you will not have it can leave you feeling guilty, depressed, anxious, and yearning for your deceased mate. You may decide consciously or unconsciously that remaining stuck in a depressive mourning is the only way you can make it up to your dead mate. You may know in your head that this doesn't make sense, but the feeling can be difficult to overcome.

Your task in getting better is to recall honestly both the strengths and weaknesses of your relationship. It is appropriate to be remorseful for failures in your relationship that were your fault. It is likely, however, that you put your dead mate on a pedestal to counter the ill-wishes you had toward him or her earlier. You may then conclude that problems in the relationship were all **your** fault. Your task will be to evaluate the relationship rationally. Ask yourself what failures in your relationship were your mate's fault? What things about your mate did you resent? What did you appreciate? How much of the responsibility should be placed on your mate? How much on you? As you answer these questions, you should be able to set aside some of your irrational guilt and therefore be more able to let go emotionally of your mate.

In summary, you are who you are, in part because of the relationship you had with your mate. You are now forever changed because of your experiences in coming to grips with the death of your mate.

You will never get "completely over" the relationship or the loss of it in your life. It is part of who you are now. Even as you eventually feel ready to begin a new life, you will not forget the past. Your task is to understand the changes that have taken place, accept them, and develop your life in the face of this new reality.

**Suggestions for Coping**

- Consider the roles and responsibilities formerly belonging to your mate, and decide which ones you must now assume and which ones are optional. You may find someone else to take over some of the optional ones. You may decide that some can be let go.

- Don't be hasty in making decisions which involve substantial sums of money. Seek out a trusted friend, relative, or professional financial advisor to help you make these decisions wisely.

- Make an effort to maintain some social relationships, even if it means discovering new groups or making friends.

- Acknowledge physical intimacy needs and look for constructive ways to take care of them. Some people find massage, by a legitimate masseuse, to be a practical solution. Pets such as dogs or cats who enjoy being stroked can also be comforting. Even taking care of a plant can involve you in intimate contact with a living thing.

- Evaluate the dependence/independence aspects of your previous marriage or relationship. If you decide you want to make changes in yourself now that you are alone, seek out the kind of help you need in identifying and accomplishing changes.

- If your relationship was conflict-ridden, work hard to realistically evaluate it. Be objective about placing the responsibility and don't take it all on your shoulders. Identify resentments and appreciations for your mate. Evaluate your own strengths and weaknesses.

- Realize that coming to grips with the killing of your mate will take courage, hard work, and patience. Getting better may take more time than you realized. Understand that you are forever changed by what has happened.

- Don't be so frightened of the pain of grieving that you try to escape it by becoming excessively active, entering into other relationships prematurely, or using large doses of medications, alcohol, or drugs. It is best to lean into the pain and fully experience it as you are able.

- Seek out support groups specifically for persons who have had a loved one killed or for persons who are widowed. You will gain hope for getting better as you see how others have survived, changed, and are coping.

- Understand that you are likely to face other losses, although hopefully not as traumatic as this one. Try to be aware of your progress in grieving the death of your mate and identify tools for coping which may help you in the future.

# NOTES

# VI

# DEATH OF A PARENT

**D**eath of a Parent During Adulthood

It is not unusual for an adult's parent to die. Most parents die before their children do. Adult children wonder about when and how their parent will die. They feel a great deal of sadness as they see their parent becoming forgetful, feeling frail, and slowing down.

Very few adult children, however, think about their parent being suddenly killed. While they may ponder over things they want to tell their parent, most adult children put them off, or at best, write them in a Mother's Day or Father's Day card. They feel pretty sure that at some time in the future, it will feel right to tell their parent how much they love and appreciate them for providing a lifetime of support and encouragement.

Nothing feels right about a parent being killed. Even if the parent was eighty-five or ninety years old, an adult child can expect the devastation described previously in this book. The killing of a parent presents some unique aspects of grieving as well.

The longer your parent lived, the more memories you have to cherish. Likewise, the more regrets you have about things you did or didn't do.

Many people regress to a child role when visiting with their parents, even if they are thirty, forty or fifty years of age. Most of us want to share our life's highs and lows with a parent. Even as adults, it is important for our parents to be proud of us.

A significant part of growing up is "cutting the apron strings," becoming independent, and directing one's own life. But even those who are most successful at doing it know that a part of them is always the child of the parent.

Thus, when a parent dies, especially if the killing was sudden and violent, an adult child can feel suddenly totally void of nurture and guidance. Your spouse holds a unique relationship with you that can be a special source of love and caring. Your child, likewise, loves you in a special way. You may become aware after your parent has been killed, that you were more nurtured than you realized. Having your parent killed may leave you feeling insecure.

Another difficult component of grief following the killing has to do with dignity. You wanted your parent to die with dignity. You wanted to be able to say that your parent lived a good full life and died easily in the presence of loved family members. That seems important based on all that your parent gave to you and others in life.

While the "time" is rarely "right" for anyone's death, it certainly doesn't seem right for your parent to die as a victim of someone's unnecessary violence or negligence. Even if your parent was in some way negligent or responsible for what happened, it does not seem right that a long life could suddenly be snuffed out in an instant. Being killed is not a dignified way to die.

A third difficult component of grief following the killing of a parent is the sudden generational role change. Before your parent died, you were the "middle generation." You had a parent or parents. You may have had a child, or at least anticipated having children some day. Suddenly, in an instant, you are the "older" generation. You may, for the first time, see your children as heirs—as you are now forced to become an heir. It is unsettling to think of yourself as the older generation. You do not feel wise enough or experienced enough to fulfill that role. Thus, even as an adult, you grieve the loss of innocence and dependence. No longer having a parent to lean on, you may feel forced into maturity before you are ready.

As is true for all kinds of death, how you respond depends on many things—how you have coped with other losses, how much emotional support you have in your grieving, and how you are getting along with those handling insurance, wills, civil and criminal procedures, and other matters. If your parent did not have a spouse and did not leave a will, you may find yourself in stressful situations with brothers and sisters about what to do with your parent's belongings.

Most of all, how you grieve depends on the relationship you had with your parent. The better the relationship, the fewer the regrets and the lesser the guilt. If you were dependent on your parent, however, you may feel more devastated and lost than others. You may experience deep longing for your parent which seems impossible to resolve. In a sense, you may feel too weak to go on without your parent.

You may experience more difficulty if you had a troubled relationship with your parent. Many children, whether they are young or adult, feel that trouble with a parent is all their fault. Even abused children sometimes spend a lifetime trying to measure up to the expectations of the parents. They believe that one day they will figure out what to do or say that will please the parent and cause the parent to feel proud of them.

If you and your parent did not get along, you may feel guilty for not trying harder to work it out. You may feel a tremendous amount of rage toward the person responsible for the killing of your parent, because your desire to make things better was made hopeless so abruptly .

If you review your past and realize that you spent a lot of time feeling bad about yourself, those hurtful feelings may resurface following the death of your parent. If you feel intensely guilty or empty because you somehow link the death of your parent with your bad feelings, you may need professional counseling. It could help you determine the rationality of your thinking process.

Most adults whose parent is killed feel some or all of the above. It is important to face all your feelings and to give yourself time in solitude to both mourn your loss and remember the positive. To do only one and not the other may be to abort part of your grieving.

Society can make it difficult for you to grieve the loss of your parent. More than any other age group, you will be expected to "get on with your life" very soon....because it is considered "natural" for adults to lose their parents.

You may be surprised to find that even your best friends will be reluctant to ask how you are or to acknowledge the difficulty of your grieving. If you were a child whose parent was killed, you would be called an orphan and persons known and unknown to you would be concerned. If your spouse were killed, you would be called a widow or widower, and friends and neighbors would be available to you, at least if you asked for help. But there is no name for the adult child whose parent has been killed. Society wants to forget quickly—even though your parent died a sudden, undignified, and unnecessary death.

## Death of a Parent During Childhood

Much has been discussed about children's grief reactions in the chapter on brothers and sisters. The reactions of children to the death of a parent and the death of a sibling overlap.

As with siblings, the impact of a parent's death on a child depends much on the child's developmental stage. Children are vulnerable to psychological problems after the death of a parent or a sibling. No one knows for sure why some children cope better than others. The quality of care-taking by the surviving parent or subsequent nurturer may be most important in how a child endures the loss of a parent.

For most children who understand that death is permanent, their initial response to the death of a parent is fear for their own survival. They can't imagine anyone but their parent putting them to bed, getting them up, feeding and clothing them. The insecurity of an adult child whose parent was killed has been discussed. For a young child, that same sense of vulnerability is much greater.

Additionally, surviving children may fear their own death. If a child's parent can disappear suddenly and without cause, so can the child.

Children tend to see their parents as all-wise and all-knowing, especially prior to adolescence. A child whose parent was killed is forced suddenly to face the reality that the parent was not wise enough or strong enough to prevent being killed. If the parent could be killed, certainly the child could also.

Guilt is a third component commonly present in grieving children. Children know they have angered the parent. They have resented the parent for disciplining them. They can wonder if the killing of the parent was their fault. If their behavior angered the parent, maybe their behavior killed the parent. If a child believes this, he may feel terribly guilty and wonder if he, too might die because of it.

Many people believe that trust is the foundation of childhood emotional development. If a child is fed when hungry, diapered when wet, nurtured when lonely, he decides, long before he can verbalize it, that life is good, the world is safe, and getting his needs met is predictable. The rest of his emotional development depends on that foundation.

The sudden death of a parent can shatter that trust, although it doesn't have to. One of the most complex components of a parent's being killed, is the fact that most or all of the adults in the family are devastated themselves. The remaining spouse, grandparents, aunts and uncles, and family friends may all be in shock and so absorbed in their own grieving that they can't reach out with assurance to the children.

If a child is shuffled from one temporary caretaker to another, he may feel emotionally "out on a limb." He may feel somewhat neglected physically and abandoned emotionally. He may no longer believe that his needs will be met. Even though he may not fully understand death, it is clear that those who surround him are weak and insecure about what they should do.

Therefore, it is important that a safe, predictable system of caring for the child be established quickly. This is not a simple task. No one can perform parenting exactly like another. But if the child knows he can trust someone to feed, clothe, bathe and love him, he can then participate in the grieving of the family. Otherwise, fears for his physical survival, withdrawal, and anger will be primary.

It is equally important for a trusted adult to explain to the child why the parent died. If the cause of the death is known, it should be discussed honestly and simply with the child within his developmental level. The caretaker should tell the truth and answer the child's questions. If it appears that the child feels guilty or is especially fearful and anxious, the fears should be elicited by questions. The child must realize that his parent's death wasn't his fault and that it will not happen to him as a result.

Misunderstandings about these issues can cause a child to be afraid and angry because his life is out of control. However, if he believes that he will be cared for, that the death was not his fault, and that he is not likely to die soon, he will probably not only endure, but develop in a healthy manner.

It must be remembered though, that as a child matures, he may have to grieve his parent's death again and again based on new developmental understandings. Life changes which are normally stressful for children may be even more difficult for the child whose parent has been killed. Adolescence, re-marriage of the surviving parent, leaving home, and facing deaths of other loved ones can be tumultuous.

## Suggestions For Adult Children Whose Parent Was Killed

- Be prepared for the fact that few if any will understand the trauma you experience when your parent is killed.

- Look for ways to honor your parent with the dignity his or her death lacked. Establish a memorial fund or trust to honor your parent. Write a memorial or poem about your parent's life and share it.

- If you had a troubled relationship with your parent, write letters to him or her to express your feelings. Write a letter to yourself from your parent, explaining how you think he or she saw the problem. These letters form a "grief work journal" that can help you adjust and heal. This could help you to decide how much guilt is appropriate. If you still find it impossible to be rational about your relationship with your parent, consider counseling.

## Suggestions For Surviving Spouses or Other Caretakers of Children Whose Parent Has Been Killed

- Maintain a routine for the child which is as stable and consistent as possible.

- Try to ensure that the mode of discipline to which the child is accustomed remains the same.

- If the surviving parent is so preoccupied with his or her own grieving that the child and his needs become an irritant, ask someone to come into the home for several weeks or months to share the parenting load. This is preferable to sending the child away which can make him feel even more abandoned and fearful.

- Avoid becoming dependent on the child for your own nurture. While your grieving can be shared and can bring you closer to each other, the child will sense your neediness if you become too dependent on him. It is too big a load for him to carry.

- Be alert to persistent fears, anxieties, guilt, or anger. Acting out behaviors such as chronic temper tantrums, clinging, or daydreaming rather than participating in school or home activities, may be cries for help. Seek counseling for your child if necessary.

## NOTES

# VII

## SUICIDE

$F$ollowing a loved one's suicide, you may feel shock, agonizing sadness, guilt, anger, and confusion, perhaps more intensely than you would ever have thought possible. While your response to the suicide may be similar to reactions to a homicide, it probably differs in several ways.

Like homicide, suicide results in the sudden, irrevocable ending of a loved one's life. You may long to have said "I love you" one more time, "I'm sorry" or "Good-bye." If a suicide note was left, you may anguish at not being able to answer it.

Teenage suicide is escalating at an alarming rate. Suicide is the third leading cause of death for fifteen to twenty-five year-olds. It is estimated that more American Vietnam War veterans have committed suicide than the 58,000 plus service personnel actually killed in combat. Elderly men are at very high risk for suicide. Knowing these facts may be of little comfort to you, however. You are probably focused on potent and bewildering feelings rather than on facts.

Some people commit suicide violently. Others choose overdoses, inhalations, or other less violent forms. How it happened and why it happened may be of great interest to those who attempt to comfort you, but what probably matters the most to you is that someone you love is no longer alive. In time you, too, will focus on the facts, but not at first.

Many people have a need to understand the whys and wherefores of a person's suicide. Being able to understand the reason for the act is to feel less vulnerable themselves. If they can conclude that it was someone else's fault, that someone "missed the signals," that a legitimate reason for the suicide existed, then it makes sense, and therefore it doesn't seem as likely to happen to themselves or to their loved ones. Try to be patient with the questions, but if you don't feel like answering them simply say, "I appreciate your interest and perhaps one day I can talk about 'how' and 'why,' but right now I'm just sad and very lonely and that's all I can deal with."

## Denial and Confusion

*There must be a mistake. He couldn't have committed suicide. He wouldn't do this to me.*

> Anne Seymour, whose close friend committed suicide.

The most devastating component of the suicide—the one which may be responsible for denial on your part—is the fact that it was your loved one's choice. It seems impossible that he or she was so miserable or felt so unloved and hopeless that suicide was seen as the only escape. Confusion and bewilderment may envelop you as you struggle to come to grips with it. You will never be able to know all the factors that contributed to your loved one's choice.

Some people take comfort in the fact that the suicide was a choice. In the midst of sadness and confusion, they find solace in the fact that the victim was "in charge" and clearly chose to end his life. If the victim was in physical or emotional torment, the suicide can even result in relief. Since no two suicides are alike, and no two responses to it are alike, only you can decide if any element of relief exists for you. If others believe that you **should** feel relieved, tell them that only you can decide how you feel.

## Anger

*I'm so mad at him that I could kill him! I'm angrier than I was at the drunk driver who killed my god-child because that guy was a stranger.*

Anne Seymour

It is not likely that your loved one committed suicide to hurt you or to get even, although that is sometimes the case. He or she likely committed suicide because no escape for anguish and torment could be imagined. The person was probably so consumed by his own sense of overwhelming physical, emotional, and spiritual pain that he simply chose to end his life to escape the pain. Or perhaps the person was withdrawn and depressed, and had developed a tunnel vision. Life's problems may have taken on overwhelming proportions and there seemed no way out. He likely became so self-focused that little thought was given to others.

In some cases, suicide is manipulative. If you sense that your loved one's suicide was committed in an attempt to prove something that could have been better proven otherwise, your anger may be ferocious. Did she mistakenly think she was unloved? Did she do this to convince you of something? Did she think she was too weak to endure disappointments or other life problems? Didn't she see how painfully unfair this would be to you? Didn't she think about the hurt and havoc you would suffer in trying to pick up the pieces? The questions go around and around in your head.

You may be angry at yourself as well. You may torture yourself by ruminating over missed signals or your perception that you didn't take the signals seriously enough. You may have thought of yourself as an aware, caring person, but now feel ashamed and degraded that you allowed this to happen. You conclude that you didn't know your loved one as well as you thought you did. How you felt about your loved one and how he felt about you are now called to question. Your self-esteem may tumble.

You may also find yourself angry at others who seem to blame you. Remember that people less close to the victim than you may be looking for answers. Often the first hypothesis reached is that you were not a good parent, spouse, lover, child or friend. How unfair! Moreover, they look to you to be able to make sense out of this senseless act. Without a doubt, even the victim could not have explained exactly why he chose to do it. Nor should such an explanation be expected of you, no matter how well you knew and loved him.

You will greatly complicate your grieving if you attempt to suppress your anger. It is a reasonable and appropriate response to what has happened, and while you may not choose to make other people miserable with your anger, you need to stay in touch with it and express it with those close to you who are able to accept your feelings. As stated previously in this book, leaning into feelings and going through them will result in relief much more quickly than suppressing them.

As time goes on and as the anger is ventilated, you will also be able to assess the situation more realistically. With the help of an accepting friend or a counselor, weigh the positive and negative attributes of your loved one as well as your relationship. Evaluate the rationality of the self-statements you make and try to discard irrational beliefs about your role in the suicide. This takes time and is hard work, so be patient with yourself.

## Guilt

If your loved one tried to reach out to you before the suicide and you weren't available, you may feel over-burdened with guilt. You may be convinced that if only you had been there, the suicide could have been prevented.

You may feel guilty for not having taken the suicide instrument from your loved one, whether it was a gun, a rope, pills or an automobile. If the suicide instrument was something you gave or purchased for the victim, you may irrationally conclude that the suicide was entirely your fault.

Those who experience some relief as a result of the suicide may feel guilty for having such a feeling. Because of religious upbringing or ethical beliefs about suicide, you may find it difficult to reconcile those beliefs with the practical components contributing to your sense of relief.

## A SURVIVOR'S EXPERIENCE

After the suicide of a loved one, one woman wrote:

*I left the hospital like a zombie, with little recollection of how I drove the thirty miles home.*

*The car soon became my "raging place." I found I could cry and scream without disturbing anyone else. So I screamed. The vocal noises sounded eerie, like a wounded wild animal. I did not know where they came from or who they belonged to, only that they needed to come out.*

*Weekly, I drove to the therapist. I passed smiling people, and wondered what there was to smile about. The "if onlys" haunted me. I felt like a rat in a Kubler-Ross laboratory. Trapped in a grief-maze with no way out, I bounded from one stage to another and back again. I made monthly pilgrimages with floral tokens to the remote hill where his ashes were scattered. I'd stand on the hill and scream, "WHY?"*

*As I sat in the Mental Health waiting room I could observe other patients and identify with their individual pain. Although I had previously done social work, this was a new chapter in empathy. "They" were no longer*

87

*separate from "me." It was "us" ...the human condition creating the common denominator.*

*It was four months before I began to let go. Suddenly, I became aware of what the inside of the therapist's office really looked like. I had never noticed the plants or the furniture, and thought that they were new.*

*I came home and put together a brick/rock pathway, and felt good for the first time in months. I remembered from somewhere that depression was blocked creativity — my sidewalk looked beautiful to me.*

*The weekly trips to the therapist lasted nine months. Eventually I saw that screaming 'why' on a hill top made no more sense than a three year old throwing a tantrum. Then one night as I was soaking in the tub, I looked up on the bathroom wall and admired a large sampler my daughter had embroidered. I had it framed years ago and thought it quite an accomplishment for a fourteen year old. Often I had read it. It was the old Serenity Prayer:*

*"God grant me the serenity to accept the things I cannot change.*

*The courage to change the things I can....*

*And the wisdom to know the difference.."*

*I mused a moment... "I wonder what the wisdom to know the difference really means?" Suddenly, it came. It meant the ability to know and accept my own limitations.*

*As badly as I had wanted it, I could not make a life choice for him. In respect for his dignity I finally allowed that he alone had made that choice, and that the choice was a human one. If humans are not perfect, then neither are their choices.... and who am I to judge? Rest in Peace. All is forgiven...finally.*

B. H. B.

Human beings have an almost innate conviction that they should be able to protect those whom they love. While that is impossible and irrational, it is difficult to shake off. You can not assume total responsibility for an act that was someone else's choice.

It is likely that little could have been done to dissuade the victim from taking his own life. If you weren't present when your loved one reached out for help, he would have sought out someone else if he truly wanted to stop himself from suiciding. If warning signals were given, they probably were couched in ambivalence. If a gun had not been available, a rope or other instrument would have been sought.

Your task in coming to grips with guilt is to transfer your focus on feelings to a focus on rational thinking. Understand that suicide is extremely complex and the suicidal act was only one component of it. Many external and internal forces merge in making suicide someone's choice.

Try to determine what proportion of the responsibility may actually have been yours. The extent is apt to be small if it exists at all. Like all human beings, you are not perfect and will need to forgive yourself for any fault which you can logically claim. You will probably find that you made the best choices you could based on the information available at the time. The greatest proportion of responsibility lies with the victim who made a choice to end his life.

## Stigma

Suicide is still little understood by the public. Some people think that only the mentally or emotionally ill commit suicide and that mental and emotional illnesses are inherited. They may conclude, therefore, that as a relative of the victim, you are also unbalanced and a poor risk for friendship. Some think that suicide is purely environmental, that you or someone else "drove" your loved one to it. You may therefore be shunned because of the incident, your family history or personal lifestyle. In order to avoid the stigma, some people choose to live a lie about the suicide. They tell others that it was an accident or death due to natural causes. While this may be comforting at first, it can greatly complicate grieving. As previously noted, much confusion surrounds the suicide experience. Choosing to lie about the suicide enhances the already existing confusion with the stress of believing one thing on the inside and telling a dissonant story on the outside.

Although it is sad that, as a family member or friend of a suicide victim, you may face ostracism, it is usually a preferable alternative to disguising the truth. Simply stated, people who live lies usually get sick. They begin to suffer physical symptoms and find themselves depressed. They do not want to talk about a cover-up and they will not be able to talk about the truth.

Talking realistically about what happened and sharing your feelings honestly with trusted and accepting friends or family members is your best prescription for recovery. A minister, priest, rabbi, or a professional counselor can be consoling, and it may be wise to pursue this kind of help even if it is not essential.

**Second Victimizations**

As newspaper reporters, coroners, insurance representatives, law enforcement officers, and lawyers probe for answers about the suicide, you may feel that your integrity and moral character are again being challenged. If you were close to the victim or if you were due an inheritance or insurance at his death, you may find yourself suspect as a murderer or an accomplice to the suicide. At the very time you need to be treated with dignity and compassion, you may have to face accusations that can enhance your guilty feelings and reap even more havoc on your self-esteem.

Regardless of your treatment, it is in your best interest to cooperate fully with these people and try to understand that their role is fact-finding. Most of them have had no training in the dynamics of bereavement following suicide, and too often they are afraid of dealing with emotions.

In order to overcome the powerlessness you may feel in facing these people, ask for documentation of their findings. Get the investigating officer's name and phone number and call from time to time until his report is complete. Ask for a written copy of the completed report and, if you see errors, call to correct them immediately.

If an autopsy was performed, obtain a copy of the report. Autopsies often unveil heretofore unconsidered rationales for the suicide such as bodies racked with pain, disease, or high concentrations of alcohol or other drugs. Not all states require autopsies on suicide victims, so don't expect one to be performed automatically. In an era when AIDS (Acquired Immune Deficiency Syndrome) is feared to an almost irrational degree, medical personnel are likely to resist autopsies in cases where a tremendous amount of blood was lost, especially if the victim was considered a high risk for AIDS.

The media can become an insatiable pest, especially if the victim was well-known in the community and if any mystery surrounds the death. You have the absolute right to refuse to talk to the media if that is your choice. Rather than responding "No comment" which may create an even more suspicious tone to the event, it is usually wise to give a one or two sentence comment such as "We are experiencing great grief because of the death of our loved one and choose to refrain from public comment at this time." Such a statement can also be written and given to the press.

The legal implications of a suicide can be extremely complex. Some insurance companies may be too eager to classify accidental deaths or homicides as suicides in order to avoid paying survivor benefits. Heirs may be eager to prove that the victim was unstable at the time recent changes in the will were made that did not benefit them. Many suicide victims leave holographic (handwritten) wills as their "final will and testament" or as a codicil (amendment) to another document. Their financial and legal matters are often in disarray as a result of depression and confusion. Various family members may be eager to handle or interpret them, each in a manner which will be the most self-serving. All of this can be frustrating to those who loved the victim and are grieving. Under these circumstances it is usually prudent for all involved in the financial or legal affairs of the victim to retain good counsel.

Sometimes a close friend was more intimately involved with the victim than family members. Friends often sense the suicidal signals, are recipients of the suicide note, and discover the body of the victim. All too often such friends are excluded from family grieving rituals and find themselves awkwardly placed in an adversarial position with the family if named as heirs in the will of the deceased. If families can be sensitive to the emotional needs of friends who are equally devastated, they too, will find support through the common bond of a grief shared.

## A Word About Surviving Children

Much of what has been written in this book about the response of children to homicide also holds true for children who experience the suicide of someone they love. Children old enough to understand what death is need to be told the truth about how it happened. Being lied to feels like being excluded from the family, especially when the truth comes out on the playground or in the neighborhood but the child knows he is not supposed to know. Children respond with guilt, anger, and confusion. Their feelings should be discussed and accepted just like those of adults.

Children sometimes believe that they were mysteriously responsible for the death of their loved one, especially if they had wished the loved one dead (as most children do from time to time, especially parents and siblings.) It is obvious that the suicide victim was distressed and unhappy. It is extremely important that children be told all they can understand about the unhappiness of the victim, so they don't assign the blame to themselves. Guilt needs to be addressed specifically. The victim did not suicide because the child was bad. The victim did not suicide because the child was not with him. The victim did not suicide because the child could have prevented it and did not.

Since children model after the adults in their lives, especially parents, they will need counteractive education and instruction about suicide. They will need to hear time and again that suicide is not a good choice for failure to solve problems, or as a way out of disappointment or depression.

## Something You Will Want to Know

There is a higher incidence of suicide in families that have experienced a previous suicide. Whether this is the first suicide, or another one, you can help prevent this from happening again. You can do this by enabling the people in your family to develop positive problem-solving strategies. It is important to build strong bonds of caring and support with each other and your religious and community groups.

### FOR MICHAEL

*Dear Michael with the dancing eyes,*
  *We wonder how your eyes got so blue -*
  *How it was that you were such a handsome lad -*
  *Why it was that you could always make us laugh.*

*We don't know.*

*We wonder why you found delight as a little boy*
  *In decorating the kitchen floor with soap*
    *Or flour or spaghetti*
      *Or covering the walls with Avon lipsticks*
      *Or filling our hearts with joy.*

*We don't know.*

*We wonder where you got the drive to hit*
  *The winning home-run,*
    *The flair to tell the funniest joke,*
      *The talent to be a fine carpenter,*
        *The compassion to love your little daughters so.*

Suicide

*We don't know.*

*We wonder about the pain in your heart,*
*If your romance with death began*
*When your brother was killed,*
*If death was your solution of choice to ease the torment,*
*If this was your final act of taking responsibility.*

*We don't know.*

*We don't know why...*
*We will never know why...*
*We don't have to know why.*

*We don't like it...*
*We don't have to like it...*
*We will never again be the same.*


*But we do have a choice about what we do with it.*
*Let us not ponder on the road not travelled -*
*Let us not become destroyed, and thereby destroy -*
*Let us not try to explain the chaos of our world.*

*Instead, let us remember*
*that memories survive,*
*that goodness lives,*
*and that love is immortal.*

Janice Lord, with grati-
tude to Beckie Brown and
Iris Bolton

## Suggestions

- Focus on your feelings rather than on the "why" and "how" at first. Understand that it is normal for you to grieve deeply and to experience confusion about what has happened.

- Understand that it is normal for you to be angry at the victim, at yourself, and even others in the aftermath of a suicide.

- As guilt becomes a problem, immerse yourself in the facts. Obtain copies of all reports, talk with witnesses, family members, and friends. This will help you regain control, and own only the portion of the blame that is reasonable. Understand that you will never discover all the answers.

- Don't let people tell you how you should feel. Your feelings are your own.

- Understand that you may be ostracized in the aftermath of the suicide and there is little you can do about it except talk openly and honestly about what happened.

- If you are involved legally or financially, retain counsel.

- Remember that the victim made the decision to commit suicide.

# NOTES

# VIII

## HOLIDAYS

*We were driving home Thanksgiving, and I was thinking about Christmas and how hard it would be. I knew we needed to get it out of our systems and cry and then have a good time. So for Christmas I gave my parents a picture of Kurt and a poem that said, "If I were here all I'd say is - I love you." We all had a good cry. This Christmas was a little better.*

*A friend sends me flowers on Kurt's birthday, It's nice to know that someone remembers and isn't afraid to remember with me.*

*The YMCA basketball program has a memorial for Kurt. I remember a card from one of Kurt's friends who had moved from the city. The card said, "Kurt, it is hard for us with you gone. We love you." Remembering is important. You still need to celebrate what their lives meant to you, even as you celebrate your own life.*

Kim Keyes, whose son, Kurt, was killed by a drunk driver.

Your family, and approximately two million others may lethargically stumble through the holidays this year—because someone they love has died during the year. If that someone was killed senselessly, coping with the holidays may be even more difficult.

Thousands whose loved one was killed more than a year ago desperately hope that this holiday will be better than the last one.

The holidays can be a cruel reminder of your deviance from the American family ideal. A heightened sense of sadness and loneliness is likely as magazines and television programs focus on intact families gathered around the holiday table or the Christmas tree to celebrate the year's most festive holidays together. Spring may be difficult because it brings Easter, signs of new life, Mother's Day, Memorial Day, Father's Day. You may feel that all your friends are abandoning you because they can't cope with you and your loss during the holidays.

As one mother said, "It seems like everyone is afraid to mention my child's name, probably because they think it will upset me. They need to understand that I will never forget, whether they mention him or not. I desperately need a way to make my child's memory a part of the holiday season. It is senseless to think that I could forget, especially at this time of year."

Support groups such as Mothers Against Drunk Driving set aside a special time during the holidays to remember their loved ones and hope for a less violent future. MADD conducts Candlelight Vigils in early December. They are simple—some music, a few brief statements, and most significantly, families coming forward to light a candle of remembrance for their loved one. Tears flow, but as one father says, "It's the loveliest way I know to say Merry Christmas and to acknowledge the joy that Janie brought to us for the seven holiday seasons we were all together."

MADD then follows its Vigils of Remembrance with numerous programs to prevent drunk driving during the holidays — red ribbons on cars to remind travelers not to drink and drive, safe-rides programs, designated driver programs, media campaigns, and others.

Families who have faced the holidays with a loved one missing and who are coping offer the following suggestions to help prevent feelings of devastation from becoming more potent than feelings of celebration. They are shared in the spirit of hope that things **will** get better. They are not given as absolutes, but are intended to trigger thoughts and ideas for each family's unique situation.

## Openly Discuss Traditions

To plan a holiday to be exactly like it has been for twenty years when a family member is missing, is to invite a traumatic event. Call the family together and make the holiday plans according to the wishes of the survivors who are hurting the most.

## Create a Special Tribute For the Day

Some families find it meaningful to light a special candle on a holiday table, put treasured remembrances on paper on a decorated table, or release helium filled balloons at sunset. Allow your own creativity to develop an appropriate memorial for your loved one.

## Plan Where to Spend the Holidays

Many people think going away will make the holidays easier. This may be helpful if "going away" means going to another family member's home, where you can be nurtured. However, If going away means trying to avoid the holiday atmosphere, remember that American holidays are celebrated throughout the country and Christmas is celebrated in many parts of the world. It is usually better to face the pain. Many families are surprised to learn that the fear of facing the holiday is worse than the holiday itself.

## Balance Solitude With Sociability

Grief is draining and solitude can help renew strength. However friends and family can be a wonderful source of support, especially if they accept you as you are and don't tell you how you should feel. If you are invited to holiday outings, make an effort to go. If there are musicals or events that you enjoyed before your loss, go to them. If you surprise yourself by enjoying them, wonderful! You may feel like crying later, but you've taken a step in the right direction.

## Relive Pleasant Memories

To go through a holiday pretending that nothing happened is a heavy burden to place on oneself. It is not only burdensome, but nearly impossible. Remember holidays past when your loved one was happy and full of life. Pick out three particularly happy memories. Celebrate and be happy for those times. If feelings of sadness pop up at inappropriate times (while at work or when a task must be completed), STOP yourself from thinking sad thoughts and think about the three happy memories you can celebrate. It won't always work, but try it.

## Set Aside Some "Letting Go" Time

Set aside on your calendar times surrounding the holiday to be alone and "let go" the sad and lonely feelings. These may be times for crying, for writing down your thoughts and feelings or pretending that your loved one is in the room with you and saying out loud some of the things you wanted to say while he or she was alive. When special times are set aside for grieving, it will be easier to postpone the flow of grief in public places where a release of emotions could be embarrassing.

## Counter the Conspiracy of Silence

Because family members generally love each other very much, they don't want to add emotional burdens to each other, and, therefore, may consciously or unconsciously conspire to avoid mentioning the person who has been killed. If this seems to be happening, take the lead by mentioning your loved one from time to time. This will alert the rest of the family that it is important to you to remember him or her and that doing so will not devastate you. Creating a special tribute or setting aside a few minutes to share memories gets it out in the open.

## Try Not to "Awful-ize"

Some people in grief conclude that "life is awful" during the holiday season. To conclude that "everything about life is now awful" is to take some awful personal experiences and generalize from them irrationally. Yes, you will have difficult times, but you can also experience some joy. Accept the love and caring of others. You can feel good if you reach out and care for someone else. Feeling good does not mean you have forgotten your loved one—or that you loved him or her less. Give yourself permission to feel sad, but also to experience joy.

## Find a Creative Outlet

Many persons in grief have a strong urge to create. If you feel creative, do something about it. Write a memorial poem or story and share it. Consider the things your loved one cared the most about and contribute to an appropriate organization or cause in his or her honor. Many families set aside the amount of money they planned to spend on holiday gifts for their loved one and buy gifts to take to a children's home, hospital, or nursing home. One mother baked gingerbread houses at Christmas time. She couldn't do it the first year after her children were killed, but the second year, and years after, she baked the houses and gave them as gifts to friends who had meant a lot to her.

## Consider the Needs of the Remaining Family

Especially concentrate on the children. Listen to them. Celebrate them. They may have deep feelings that will be overlooked if you focus on yourself. Getting out Christmas tree ornaments one by one and decorating the tree can be a draining emotional experience when you are grieving. The temptation may be great to "forget it." But consider the importance of the Christmas tree and gifts to the children. A friend or relative will likely be more than happy to decorate your tree and help with purchasing and wrapping gifts if you cannot.

101

## Utilize Available Resources

Persons of religious faith are encouraged to utilize their church, synagogue, or other community of faith in coping. Some "veterans of faith" have a serenity, a quiet presence, a kind of healing wisdom. Seek them out for the support and wisdom their presence offers. You may wish also to seek out a support group of persons who have suffered similar losses. The Mental Health Association in most communities will have a list of available support groups. Or establish you own short term support group to help get through the holidays. The most valuable helper is usually someone who shares a common loss, one who understands something of what you're going through. Spend as much time as possible with the person(s) you love most.

Most important, remember that you can't change the past. You can take charge of the present, however. And you can shape the future. Total recovery may never come. But what you make of the ashes of your trauma is up to you.

*Our Michael's birthday was December 22. He was killed on February 4. So that time is very emotional. The first Christmas of my married life was spent in the hospital with my own 'babe'. Now, six years later, we still hurt, but we go on. Each December 22, Mike's brothers have a pizza party in his memory. When he would have been 22, nine of his friends got together on the 22nd and ate 22 pieces of pizza. What a marathon!*

Rita Chiavacci

# IX

## SPIRITUALITY

*"I no longer believe that God is a 'good' God."*

*"You'll never see me darken the door of a church again."*

*"Only my faith in God has enabled me to endure this."*

*"If one more person tells me that God needed another flower in his garden, I'm going to throw up."*

Even if you rarely thought about God before your loved one was killed, you have probably heard the word "God" and contemplated about God in relation to the death.

A minister, priest, or rabbi may have officiated at the funeral of your loved one. You may have received faith-oriented sympathy cards. Friends and relatives may have attempted to comfort you with references to God. When death comes, like it or not, most families deal with "God."

Some people experience God as a personal supporter, a presence bigger than life which gives them strength and peace. They say that their faith in God sustains them as they endure their suffering.

Other people are angry at God. They believe that they were faithful religious people and God let them down by allowing their loved one to be killed.

*"I feel so bad. I just can't comprehend it, it's so horrible,"* *I wrote three months after John was killed. All I can say* *is "Oh my God, Oh my God." I feel like I'm going to* *split into pieces. Why did God let this happen? If there's* *a God, I hate Him.*

Margaret Grogan, Whose son was murdered.

Others are confused and frustrated with the things people say about God. They wonder why, in the trauma of staring an ugly death in the face, anyone would dare talk about "eternal life" or "heaven" as if that should take all the tears away.

Friends, relatives, and even the clergy may say religious things which can hurt more than help. Almost always, these people mean well. They want to help you feel better. They may not know how. Or, more likely, they may not understand that feeling better is probably not possible for some time, and that all you really want is for them to join you in your suffering. It is also possible that you might misunderstand what others mean when they talk about God.

## "It Was God's Will"

This "consolation" may cause more pain to victim families than any other well-intended phrase. A sudden, violent death is absurd. Your loved one didn't deserve it. You don't deserve it. Therefore, for God to have willed it makes no sense.

In your pain, you may cry out, "Why? Why?" even though you understand the cause of the killing. You long for a better explanation, a deeper, more profound reason.

It is paradoxical that the more you long for an answer to the mysterious "why," the more difficult it is to find answers. The cause of a tragic death is usually someone's choice or negligence. It is a "human being" problem rather than a "God" problem. As long as humans have the freedom to make choices, some will choose to be evil at worst, negligent at best; and the innocent will suffer the consequences.

Into the midst of your turmoil about the "why," a well-meaning person may tell you that the tragedy was "God's will." Such a person implies that a mystical reason was responsible for your loved one's death, but the reason was known only to God. They imply that the reason is beyond understanding. Only you can decide if that reasoning makes sense.

If this line of reasoning doesn't make sense and is unacceptable, you will probably feel angry and resentful about the explanation. You may identify with the Jewish leader who responded, "Oh, I hope not," when asked if there was a meaning to the holocaust.

Why, then, do people so often use the phrase, "It was God's will?" It is an easy answer to questions they don't understand.

Persons who relate to you after the killing of your loved one are usually nervous and anxious. They want to be helpful. They want you to feel better, but may not think before speaking.

When a child asks, "Why is the grass green?" it's easy to respond, "That's the way God made it." When the grass turns brown and looks dead, it's easy to give the same response. It quiets the child and provides an escape for the parent who may not know the scientific answer to the question.

The role of a Higher Being in what happened to you is your own faith decision. If you believe that somehow it was "God's will" that's fine. If it doesn't make sense, try to understand that those who say it mean well. They may be sharing their own faith decision and are not trying to hurt you.

## "It's Sinful to be Angry"

Perhaps you grew up being told that it was bad to feel or display anger. Just as Santa Claus or the Easter bunny might not come if you were "bad" or acted angry, so would God reject you if you felt angry.

It is amazing that so many people believe that anger is bad when most religions address anger as a significant component in fighting or counteracting evil. So, why are some people so eager to tell you piously that you shouldn't be angry?

They probably do it because they fear you might do violent deeds as a result of your anger. The thought of a suicide or homicide on your part, in response to the killing of your loved one, would be the ultimate trauma to those who love you. They would feel better if you assured them of your rationality. Just because you feel rage, revenge, or fantasize about "doing in" the offender, doesn't mean that you are a vigilante.

It is extremely rare that persons deeply in grief make serious plans to kill the offender. They may think about it, but they very rarely commit a hostile or criminal act.

If your friends are so agitated about your anger that they feel compelled to try to stop your angry feelings, assure them that no harm will come to the offender or yourself. If you believe that the Higher Being of your faith can handle your anger, rage, thoughts about revenge, and confusion, tell them. You will feel better if you do, and so will they.

> *Help! I can't stand this anymore! Get me out of*
> *here, God!*

> *The mud of my distress*
> *Has sapped my strength,*
> *Disrupted my belief,*
> *Drowned my faith.*

*Where are you, God?*
*Why won't you rescue me*
*From this mire?*

*Move over.*

*I don't promise to remove you*
*from the pain of living.*
*But I do ask you to give me room*
*To sit in the mud beside you.*

*Remember my promise to never leave you?*
*Trust me.*
*Move over.*

Dorothy Mercer

## "You Must Forgive"

Without a doubt, you will be called upon to rethink your concept of forgiveness after a loved one has been killed. And if you're going to survive the trauma without keeping your stomach tied in knots for years, you will need to decide how you can' deal with the offender and maintain your integrity.

In killings in which the offender was also killed, the issue of forgiveness can be avoided somewhat. For those in which the offender is alive, especially if the criminal justice system is involved in the case, the issue cannot be avoided.

Society tends to forgive easily. It is so eager to forgive that it doesn't require remorse on the part of the offender. Many homicides are plea-bargained in the criminal justice system with offenders being advised by their attorney to "plead guilty" to a lesser offense in return for more lenient sentences. At the same time, the offender is instructed not to make contact with the victim family because it might imply an admission of guilt. Does society and the criminal justice system really believe that such a plea is genuine remorse? Apparently so, because it is all that is required.

107

Your family may say, "If only he would look me in the eye and genuinely say 'I'm sorry.' it would mean all the world to me." The common response to such a statement is that "only a vengeful family would put an offender through that." To you it may be a very significant component in justice with integrity.

Some victim families, when shown genuine remorse by an offender, have offered forgiveness even though they can never forget. Many cannot forgive. Most are unwilling to offer a "cheap grace" to offenders—a gesture of forgiveness which has no real meaning because the offender has shown no remorse and made no commitment to a change in behavior.

You will need to decide, based on your own life experiences and religious convictions, what to do about forgiveness. It is a difficult task. If others imply that you should offer forgiveness, tell them it is an important matter and that you will handle it in a manner that your integrity allows.

## "If You Just 'Turn It Over to God,' You'll Be All Right"

Some may suggest that God is like a tranquilizer who will smooth the rough edges if you have enough faith. To make such a difficult task sound so simple may irritate you. Perhaps you have prayed, but your prayers did not seem to be answered. Or you may have prayed and found a sense of calm and peace, but you are still confused. Veterans of faith in most religions find something of an "abiding presence" in the midst of their longing and suffering. They experience their God or Higher Being not so much as a solution to their problem of grief, as a Companion who stands with them in the midst of it. That kind of faith gives strength.

Because most of the people who love you feel inadequate in helping you feel better, they wish that God would do it for them. They especially wish that their God would be present in you. Thus, words which may sound overly simplistic and trite, actually may be expressions of their own genuine concern.

You may or may not believe that the soul of your loved one lives on in eternity. If you do, that, in itself, is consoling. It does not mean, however, that you don't have the right to miss and deeply long for the body and presence which you no longer can see, hear, or touch. Perhaps it will be helpful to you, as well as those who attempt to comfort you, to explain that there are many components of grieving and that you are dealing with the religious components as honestly as you can.

*Recently I asked Elie Wiesel how to overcome despair. We had been talking about things touching on despair, and on God. Hence my question. This man, who, more than most, has reason to despair, this man who lost his family in the death camp and himself barely survived, looked at me with those deep, dark eyes that have looked into the abyss and said, "You want to know how to overcome despair. I will tell you. By helping others overcome despair."*

*He waited, then smiled a small smile. I realized the truth of what he'd said because I was feeling less despair in that moment precisely because he and I had talked together, shared together our struggles. He was saying that in that, I had helped him with his despair even as he helped me with mine. Eternal life and whatever hints at it is something we cannot have alone, only together.*

Theodore Loder, Pastor
First United Methodist
Church of Germantown,
Philadelphia

## After-Death Spiritual Experiences

Mystical experiences are fairly common among those whose loved one has died. They can be very spiritually and emotionally healing to those fortunate enough to have them.

Loved ones report having received direct and spontaneous communications from their deceased loved ones which range from a vague sense of the presence of the person who died to hearing voices, seeing visions—transparent figures to full bodies, feeling touches, and smelling aromas such as the loved one's perfume or after shave. Verbal or unspoken communications frequently center on "I'm okay," "Don't grieve for me," "I love you," or a derivative of "Goodbye."

No one knows for sure if these reported occurrences are true messages from the deceased or merely coincidences which were assigned meaning because the receiver needed to find meaning in them. It is clear, though, that they offer reassurance and comfort to surviving loved ones.

If you have had such an experience, accept it and celebrate it in whatever way you find meaningful. Share it with a few people you can trust. You will probably be surprised at the number of people who have had something similar happen to them.

This phenomenon is discussed openly in many cultures around the world. Our society is so scientifically oriented that we easily lose touch with the mystical.

On the other hand, try not to despair if you have not had this kind of experience. No one knows why some do and why some don't.

All of these issues of faith are a part of your grief process. Processing them takes time and effort. By engaging them you are working through your loss.

## Suggestions:

Following are some guidelines for dealing with the religious dimensions of your suffering.

- Look for someone who has had an experience similar to yours who also has a meaningful religious faith. If you feel comfortable doing so, ask that person how their faith is helpful to them. You may or may not be able to share their experience.

- Avoid discussion with religious people who use God as a simple answer to complex questions. Try to accept the fact that their faith journey may have been different from yours.

- Avoid conflict with religious people who are not comfortable with your anger and range of feelings. Assure them that you will not harm yourself or others as a result of your feelings.

- Try reading a few chapters from the Book of Psalms in the Bible—perhaps Psalms 23 and 139. Write in a journal or notebook what they mean to you.

- If you continue to be troubled about religious feelings or beliefs, contact a hospital chaplain or a counselor of your religion. These people have had special training in accepting and dealing with grief. Or you can seek out a pastor, priest or rabbi who has previously been helpful to you or others.

# NOTES

# X

## PROFESSIONAL COUNSELING

It is not easy to decide if or when you need the help of a professional counselor in coping with your grief. Many people find that going to counseling is helpful even if they feel they could get along without it. Counseling certainly won't hurt you if your counselor has some understanding of trauma following the killing of a loved one and is committed to treating survivors with dignity and compassion.

As previously discussed, grief has many of the same symptoms as clinical depression:

- Appetite changes
- Sleep disturbances
- Physical complaints
- Decreased sexual desire
- Loss of energy
- Inability to concentrate
- Need to withdraw

These normal symptoms of grief following tragic loss can be misdiagnosed, if the counselor is not fully aware of what you have been through.

Over the years additional symptoms have been found that commonly occur in survivors which should be considered normal based on the trauma experienced. These include:

- Unanticipated periods of crying which recur for years (grief spasms).
- Dreams and flashbacks from time to time.
- Anger which is difficult to focus.
- Difficulty deciding what to do with mementos, clothing and other "things" of the deceased.
- Deep sadness, including death wishes accompanied by irrational thinking, homicidal or suicidal fantasies.
- Fear and anxiety, particularly about getting out in the community alone.

It is rarely, if ever, appropriate to look at grief from the medical model, i.e., "You are sick and therefore require treatment to get well again." It is more appropriate to look at the severity of the trauma that caused the symptoms, and then decide whether or not they are normal reactions to a very abnormal event.

No one knows for sure how long you should grieve, how many symptoms you should expect, or how intense a particular symptom will be for you. We do know that for most people, the grieving is painful and it lasts a long time.

It is even difficult to decide what word to use in thinking about what it means to feel better.

"Recovery" sounds like you were sick and became well again. Very few people who have had someone they love killed ever feel completely "recovered." Most say they are changed by their loss.

Many survivors rejuvenate on their own if they have family and friends who accept and support them and join them in their grieving. People in grief need to talk about the circumstances of the killing and memories of their loved one over and over again. It is a way of coming to grips with it.

If family and friends support you through this, you are fortunate because they will play a major role in your improvement. If family and friends are unable or unwilling, you can find support in grieving from organizations which provide grief support groups. Many survivors spend months or years in a support group as they regain emotional health. If none of these are available, you may decide to seek professional help. Or you may choose to procure professional help along with the help of support groups.

Most people know when they require professional help. They know because their physical symptoms are severe or because they are not improving. Some know they need help because their emotional pain is too difficult to endure. A professional can help you assess whether what you are thinking or feeling is appropriate to your loss and grief at a particular stage of your bereavement. It is paradoxical that sometimes when you are feeling unsure, you are actually progressing through your grief nicely.

The remainder of this chapter can serve as a checklist for you in deciding about professional help. Following are some of the symptoms which indicate that you may need some counseling and/or **short-term** prescription medication to help you to feel better. After a period of professional help, you may find that friends, family, and/or a support group are sufficient.

## Getting "Stuck" in Grief

Grieving the loss of a loved one to a violent and unanticipated death continues, to some degree, for years. But if you look over the last several months or years and see that your grief symptoms are just as intense now as they were then, that you're not even a little better, you may be "stuck." The pain of having a loved one killed takes a while to surface. It is more intense and lasts longer than the pain of an anticipated and non-violent death. If you can't look back and see that you are

115

getting better, or can't imagine ever feeling better in the future, you may need professional help.

## Absence of Grief

It is true that not all people grieve openly. Some people seem able to take trauma in stride. They may carry on, busy and efficient, and appear to be coping splendidly. It is wise, however, if you are one of these persons, to look carefully and sensitively at yourself. Do you feel anxious when you think of the one who was killed? Are you uncomfortable when friends offer sympathy? Do you forbid others to talk about your deceased loved one? Are you more tense and short-tempered than you were before?

Nearly all people grieving the killing of a loved one go through a period of denial when nothing about the death seems real. That is normal. In time, reality sinks in. Though difficult, it is healthy to lean into the pain and not fight it.

You may believe that it is bad to think about your dead loved one because the pain will be intolerable. You may fear losing control. If you are "carrying on as usual," but find that it takes a lot of energy to keep yourself from thinking about your dead loved one or to keep others from reminding you, you may need the help of a professional in deciding to face your grief and loss.

## Pre-existing Problems

If you had problems coping with your life before your loved one was killed, it is likely that those problems will increase. Health problems may get worse. If you have a history of mental or emotional problems, they may get worse. If your family or your marriage suffered problems, they may get worse. If you were a "loner" and didn't attract people to support you before, you will probably have difficulty finding support now.

Sudden death in a dysfunctional family can be complex. Families in which a parent abuses alcohol or other drugs, families in which physical or sexual abuse are common, and even families in which one or both parents are workaholics are families in which denial reigns as a style of life. People pretend that what's going on isn't really going on. In most cases, these adults suffered deep hurts as children, but because the hurts were so painful, they learned to deny them. They learned to pretend. In fact, the worse things were at home, the better they looked and acted in public.

These same unspoken rules "Don't feel what you feel," "Don't talk about your pain," "What happens in the family is the family's business and no one else's," can be extremely detrimental in acknowledging and leaning into grief. For many, a courageous and painful journey back to childhood will be required before the present grief can be faced. Under stress, most people resort to their lowest level of functioning, and what members of a dysfunctional family do best is stay in control to cover up pain. That is exactly the opposite of what is required for grief work.

These facts need not discourage you. They simply mean that if you had problems in your family before the death, you are more likely to need professional help than others who do not have these factors in their lives. You must take responsibility to seek the help you and your family need.

### Negative Self-Concept

Self-esteem can suffer a hard blow when sudden violent death invades a family. Many survivors feel guilty and blame themselves for what happened. Most feel inadequate in trying to comfort others. Most wonder if they are strong enough to survive their grieving.

In time, however, with a healthy dose of rational thinking, survivors are able to place responsibility appropriately. If you can't do that, if you feel that you are bad and incompetent and to blame, you probably need to talk these perceptions through with a counselor. Negative self-concepts, especially if they have been present a long time, and grief are a formidable combination. You deserve help in coming to grips with them.

## Excessive Guilt

Guilt, as we have noted before, is normal for awhile in grieving. If your relationship with the one who was killed was good, you will likely be able to resolve your guilt in time. You will be able to remember the good times along with the bad times.

If, however, your relationship with the one who was killed was troubled, your guilt may consume you. It can be so devastating that your conscience shoves it underground and forgets the bad times. Then, the hostility is no longer felt and the one killed is placed on a pedestal. This phenomenon may happen when a teenager or parent of a teenager is killed because negative feelings are common as adolescents break away from the family. They may happen when one partner in a troubled marriage is killed.

Sometimes, the guilt can be so severe that the survivor keeps the victim mentally alive in order to cope. In such cases, the deceased is referred to as if he or she were still alive. Most survivors have nightmares and flashbacks from which they emerge wondering if the victim really is dead. That is normal. But the person needing professional help will believe, all the time, that their loved one is still alive.

Sometimes the survivor needs continuing communication with the deceased so much that he devises magical rituals to communicate. It is normal for survivors to need weeks or months before they are able to sort through the clothing and room or house of their loved one. But people deeply in distress can make a "shrine" of the things and room of their loved one. Such a person wants the room left **exactly** as it was before and becomes enraged if anyone attempts to move anything. This survivor might attach magical significance to the room and touch certain things or look at particular objects as a means of seeking some kind of attachment to the deceased. A skilled counselor understands why a survivor finds it necessary to respond in this manner and will gently and patiently help the survivor to face both the good and the bad and to grieve appropriately.

## Dependency

Losing someone upon whom you are very dependent is extremely traumatic.

A child whose parent has been killed cannot easily transfer dependence to a new caretaker.

The elderly parent who depends on his adult child for care can be devastated by losing the child.

The spouse who relies on the mate for physical functions, instruction, comfort, and support will be filled with stress, fear, and anxiety when forced to go it alone.

Some parents depend heavily on their child to fulfill their needs. A mother can feel that she is important only because her child needs her. Obviously, she will have a very difficult time coping if her child is killed.

Social support from family and friends and a transfer to others who can be counted on are essential for a dependent survivor to get better. If they are not available for you, give yourself a break and find a counselor to help you find yourself again and learn a new way to live.

## Suicide

Suicidal thoughts are not uncommon among the bereaved. As denial and shock give way to painful physical symptoms, to deep anger, and to great sadness, many survivors say they, too, long to die to escape the pain and/or to be reunited with their loved one. Most of them, however, will think rationally about the consequences of suicide and look for a more constructive way to cope. One mother's despair overcame her to the degree that she took a gun to her daughter's grave, planning to commit suicide. As she swept the dry snow from the headstone, she became keenly aware that she didn't believe she would ever see her daughter again in Eternity if she killed herself.

If your despair goes beyond a desire to simply not wake up in the morning and you become pre-occupied with the idea of killing yourself, you must seek professional help. If you find yourself unable to think rationally and have devised a plan for your own demise, you **must** tell someone. A counselor can help you find other ways to relieve the pain.

If you seriously contemplate suicide, you may find that your mind is focused on the one who is likely to discover your body. You may be very angry at that person and contemplate using the suicide to hurt him or her. A counselor can help you discover other ways of handling that problem.

If you have made up your mind to commit suicide, it will take strength and courage on your part to change your mind. For the sake of those who love you, you must stop yourself until you have at least visited a counselor to help you consider other alternatives.

**Finding a Good Counselor**

It is sad but true that not all counselors or psychotherapists are skilled at grief therapy following a violent and unanticipated death. Therefore, you may need to shop around for the right counselor.

Word of mouth is still the best referral source. Call the support groups in your community to find other survivors and inquire about the names of helpful counselors. There are many non-profit counseling and support groups such as Compassionate Friends, Parents of Murdered Children, MADD, Hospice, and Mental Health agencies. They can provide support or give you referrals to grief counselors.

After obtaining counselor names, call several and ask the following questions:

1. Have you ever worked with clients who have had a loved one killed? How many?

2. What kind of counseling do you do with people deeply in grief?

120

3. Under what circumstances do you arrange for prescription drugs?

4. About how many sessions do you have with a client who is having problems with grief?

5. What licenses or certifications do you have?

6. How much continuing education have you received during the last few years? Have you had any training in grief therapy?

7. Do you provide only one-on-one counseling or do you have victim support groups as well?

8. How much do you charge? Do you take insurance? Do you have a sliding scale?

The most important rule in finding a counselor who can help you is to **trust your "gut" feelings**. If, after two or three sessions, you do not feel supported, understood and comfortable, you have the right to go elsewhere.

Parts of therapy are painful. But a good counselor will support you as you go through the pain. You will find yourself looking forward to the sessions because you trust that your counselor will treat you with dignity and compassion. If that does not happen, look elsewhere.

# NOTES

# XI

## COPING WITH CRIMINAL JUSTICE SYSTEM

You may think that coming to grips emotionally with the killing of your loved one is your sole task. Unfortunately, it is not.

After most killings, the offender will be apprehended. In some murders and in hit-and-run vehicular crashes, the offender will never be found. This situation adds another component to the grieving of surviving family and friends. The need for fairness and justice is totally thwarted in these cases and can mean more complicated grieving. It is difficult to focus anger when no one is clearly responsible. Feelings of helplessness and hopelessness can emerge. The anger can easily, if not always appropriately, be focused on law enforcement agencies who cannot locate the offender.

When the offender is also killed, survivors report mixed emotions. Some feel a sense of relief although this does not diminish the grief for their loved one. Others feel it would have been better for the offender to be dealt with by the criminal justice system.

If the offender was not killed and was apprehended, you are now involved with the criminal justice system. It is against the law to kill someone, intentionally, maliciously or with criminal negligence. Therefore, the State has a responsibility to prosecute the offender for the commission of a crime and attempt to obtain a conviction.

As the surviving family, you probably are interested in obtaining justice and seeing the offender punished, even though no sentence seems "just" or adequate for what was done to your loved one.

The word "State" is significant. Your family is not a party to the criminal suit. The style of the criminal legal documents does not read "Victim Name v. Offender Name," but "The State v. Offender Name." Unless you were present when your loved one was killed and, therefore, an eye witness to the offense, you will not automatically be involved in the case.

Most victim families find the detachment of the criminal justice system personnel extremely frustrating. You may say, "It was not my State that was killed. It was my loved one!"

That is true, but the role of the State is to punish the offender because he broke the law. You will learn more about what you personally can do in suing the offender civilly in the next chapter.

*I can accept a great deal of ignorance and a great deal of lack of awareness—but to be told that I am not a real victim when I have lost something that is more precious to me than my own life, I will not tolerate. If you feel you are not dealing with real victims when you deal with homicide survivors, just call me.*

Dorothea Morefield,
whose son was murdered.

However, within the last few years, the criminal justice system has, in most jurisdictions, become more involved with the victim family. A recent U.S. Supreme Court case upheld the right of victims to testify about the impact of the crime on their lives at sentencing trials, even in death penalty cases. Crime victim families now have some statutory rights, in all 50 states, although victims are still not a party to the criminal law suit.

Don't get too excited, however. While such laws are now in place, no sanctions exist for the prosecutor or representatives of the State who neglect to grant the victim family their rights. Since many of the rights are on paper only, you may have to be assertive in order to claim them.

*When my son was kidnapped, brutally beaten to death, and twice robbed, neither the law enforcement nor the justice system acknowledged the existence of survivors of homicide victims, let alone allowed them any rights.*

*Though such sloppy treatment is not as widespread today as it was then, there remains considerable, die-hard resistance to the rights of survivors even in those states where legislation provides for them. There is little or no recourse to that resistance and no effective reprimands for those who "forget" to extend said rights.*

Janet Barton

## What Can You Do?

### The Crime Report

The crime report is prepared by the law enforcement agency who investigated the killing of your loved one. It is usually the City Police Department if the crime happened within city limits. Generally, the County Sheriff's Department investigates crimes outside the city limits. In the case of highway crashes outside the city limits, the State Highway Patrol takes charge of the investigation. Call the appropriate agency and ask how and when you can receive a copy of the report. Typically, a supplemental report will be filed after more investigation has been done. Ask if, how, and when you may obtain copies of the supplemental reports.

The investigating officer should give you the identification number of the report. If not, or if you lost it, you can obtain the report by giving the date and scene of the crime. Knowing the offender's name is helpful, but not essential. Look the report over closely for the following data:

- Do you see errors in the report? If so, report them immediately to the investigating officer whose name is at the bottom of the report. Even if they seem minor, they can be crucial to court cases.

- Are there any indications on the report that the offender had been drinking or using drugs when he killed your loved one? If so, see if a Blood Alcohol Content (B.A.C.) level is indicated on the crime report. B.A.C. is usually determined by breath, blood, or urine testing shortly after the crime was committed. If the tests were not performed, you have the right to know why they were not.

- These tests should be routinely given following automobile crashes in which drug/alcohol abuse is suspected. Valid B.A.C. testing can result in tougher penalties and sentences for drunk drivers.

- Blood alcohol and drug testing is not as routinely given in other homicide cases because of the usual lapse of time between committing the crime and apprehension of the offender. In many states, the consumption of alcohol/drugs before or during the crime, if it is not a vehicular crime, is considered a **mitigating** circumstance which may result in a more lenient sentence.

## The Investigating Agency (Police, Sheriff, State Trooper)

- Ask what charges are being recommended, why they were selected, and what elements of proof will be necessary to expect a conviction.

- Ask when the investigating agency is likely to transfer the case to the prosecutor's office (sometimes referred to as the county attorney, the district attorney, or state's attorney). Leave your name and phone number and ask to be notified when the case is transferred. If you have not heard from them within a few days after they planned to transfer the case, call to ask the case status.

- Ask if the investigating agency has a victim advocacy program. It is the victim advocate's role to keep you informed of the status of the case and to provide services you may need as a crime victim. Services include referrals to appropriate agencies, victim counseling, and assistance in applying to the State Victim Compensation Program for reimbursement for uninsured expenses resulting from the victimization.

- If you are not satisfied with the information the investigation officer or victim advocate has given, ask to speak with the investigating officer's supervisor.

## Evidence

You may assume that the investigating officers have collected all the evidence they need. However, it is wise to document everything about the crime **at the time it comes to your attention**. You think you'll remember all the facts, but documentation will ensure a good recollection of all details.

- Additional witnesses may come forth who were not interviewed by the investigating officer. If so, refer them to the officer or to the prosecutor who will take their statement.

- Investigators have probably taken pictures at the crime scene and at the medical examiner's office. It is possible, however, that other pictures would be useful in both the criminal and civil case. A recent picture of your loved one before he or she was killed may be presented to the court prior to sentencing. It will personalize your loved one who is unknown to the court. If you take pictures after the crime was committed that you think may be helpful, have someone witness your taking the photographs. You and the witness should sign and date the photos on the back, and take them to the prosecutor.

- Ask for the return of clothing or personal effects of your loved one which may be in the investigator's office, the hospital, or the medical examiner's office. Some of them may need to be retained for the trial, but you should be given those that are not essential to the case. Ask about the condition of these things before opening the container to look at them.

- Begin a record or log with receipts and bills of all financial expenditures involved in the killing of your loved one. These may include medical and funeral expenses, lost wages, fees for hiring a private investigator, and costs of counseling for the surviving family. This information will be critical if the offender is found guilty and the judge orders him to pay restitution to your family. It is also necessary in filing for State Crime Victim's compensation, insurance benefits, and civil suits.

## The Prosecutor

After the investigating officer has transferred the case to the County Attorney, District Attorney, or State Attorney, find out which prosecutor has been assigned to your case. Information will be filed under the defendant's name. Let the prosecutor know that you want to be informed of what is happening during all stages of the criminal justice process. In most states, you will not be informed unless you specifically request this. Therefore, the prosecutor and/or the victim advocate should be notified in person or by phone of your desire to be informed. Make a note of all your calls.

A follow-up letter should be mailed to both the prosecutor and the victim advocate stating the name of the accused, your name, address, and phone number, your desire to be informed, the facts as you understand them about the case, and any feelings you have about bail for the accused, plea bargaining, or any other aspect of the case. Ask in your letter to be informed if the prosecutor charges the offender any differently from the investigator's recommendation.

## Understand Charging

After reviewing the evidence in the case, the prosecutor may:

- Issue the criminal charges recommended by the investigating agency;
- Issue different, fewer, or additional charges; or
- Decide not to issue charges because of insufficient evidence.

In most states, one of two procedures will be used to determine whether probable cause or sufficient evidence exists to proceed to trial.

- A preliminary hearing may be held in which the prosecutor and possibly a few witnesses appear before the judge. If the judge determines that sufficient evidence exists, the accused will be scheduled for arraignment.

- A grand jury hearing is much the same as a preliminary hearing except the evidence is presented by the prosecutor to a group of citizens rather than to a judge. Most grand juries are composed of citizens who serve for several months at a time. Grand jury proceedings are closed to the public (including the victim's family). The accused is not present while others testify. The accused may or may not be called to testify. If the grand jury determines that sufficient evidence exists, they hand down a true bill of indictment. If they do not think that sufficient evidence exists, the case is "no-billed." If indicted by the grand jury, the accused will be scheduled for arraignment.

## Arraignment

At the arraignment, the accused appears personally before a judge who informs him of the charges pending and of his constitutional rights, including the right to a court-appointed defense attorney. The accused is now called the defendant and will enter a plea of guilty or not guilty.

## The Defense Attorney

The attorney for the defendant or one of his investigators may phone, write or appear on your doorstep. Before you communicate with **any** attorney or investigator, confirm his identity. Ask who he represents. A defense attorney is **not** a District Attorney even though he may refer to himself as a D.A. The defense attorney clearly is not there to represent your rights as a victim.

You do not have to speak to the defense attorney or investigator unless subpoenaed to do so. Ask him to get the requested information from the prosecutor's office. The prosecutor will accompany you if you are subpoenaed to give a deposition (statement) under oath.

## Bail or Bond Hearing

Sometimes bond is set at the arraignment. Sometimes it is set at a separate hearing. Bail or bond is an amount of money given to a court by the defendant in exchange for his release and his promise to appear in court. The defendant can usually post bond through a bonding company for about 15% of the actual amount of bond set. It can be very important for a representative of the victim family to be present when bond is set. This representative can inform the court of relevant facts concerning the defendants likelihood to abscond or the danger to your family if he is released. This information could result in a higher bond or refusal of bond for a dangerous offender.

## Discovery/Preliminary Hearings

After arraignment, the prosecutor and the defense attorney will gather evidence to support their cases. If the defendant has been arraigned on charges you don't understand, ask the prosecutor to explain to you the elements which must be proven to get a conviction. Discuss the strengths and weaknesses of the case. If you understand these, you may be able to provide additional information which will be helpful to the prosecution of the case. You may know of additional witnesses or have ideas about beneficial evidence. The prosecutor should know that you support him in trying to convict the defendant on the highest charges that can be proven.

## Continuances

Ask to be informed of pre-trial hearings including requests for continuances. Pre-trial hearings are open to the public (including you) even though attorneys usually tell you it is unnecessary for you to be there. Defense attorneys usually request numerous "continuances"—or postponements to "age the case." They know that the longer they can postpone trial, the more likely the state will lose its witnesses, and witnesses' memories will fade. Be sure the prosecutor vigorously opposes unnecessary continuances at every opportunity.

In some states, the prosecutor may request a speedy trial on the basis of sensitivity to victims. (Defendants have a constitutional right to a speedy trial, but it is rarely in their interest to request it, especially if they have been released on bond.) Also, in some states the judge is required to state in the record the reason for granting a continuance.

Continuances may be requested by the State or by the defense. They are often for legitimate reasons—work conflicts, unavailability of witnesses, etc. They do not necessarily mean that your case is being ignored.

Ask the prosecutor or victim advocate if you have the right to be informed of pre-trial hearings and to provide input into them. If you do have the rights in your state, claim them. Do your best to see that your case is not disposed of without your knowledge.

## Plea Bargaining/Sentence Bargaining

These terms refer to negotiations which take place between the prosecutor and the defense attorney. These negotiations may result in a plea to a lesser charge or to a particular sentence in exchange for a reduced sentence. Bargains are usually distasteful to victim families who feel that to "cut a deal" is to betray the significance of the killing of their loved one, although this is not always the case.

In some circumstances, plea/sentencing bargaining is beneficial. If the preliminary investigation was inadequate, the offender may have been arraigned on a charge the State cannot now prove. It is better to allow the defendant to plead guilty to a lesser charge and be punished for it than to go to trial and lose everything.

Many states now require that the victim's family be informed if plea or sentence bargains are considered. A few states allow the victim's family the right of input into bargaining decisions. Know your rights and assert yourself in claiming them. It is very important that you be present if a plea is presented to the judge. It will remind him that both the victim and the defendant should be considered in the decision rendered.

**Victim Impact Statements**

All states except Hawaii have enacted laws or procedures which allow for the victim family to give a written or oral statement to the court about the impact of the crime on their lives. These statements are presented after the defendant has been convicted.

Most judges require the Adult Probation Department of their county to conduct a Pre-Sentence Investigation (PSI) on a defendant to collect information about what kind of sentence would be most appropriate. A convicted offender may be sent to jail for a certain number of days, or to state prison for few or many years. If the sentence is probated, (served outside jail or prison), conditions of probation can vary widely. He may or may not be required to pay fines to the State. He may or may not be required to pay restitution to the victim family. He may or may not be required to attend counseling, or a number of other options probation officers may recommend.

Until recently, pre-sentence investigations focused solely on the offender. The victims movement has succeeded in convincing many state legislatures that unless the victim perspective is **also** presented, the court has not heard the whole story. The advent of Victims Impact Statements is a tangible result of this movement.

It is very important that Victim Impact Statements be prepared and presented to both the prosecutor and the probation department **before** a hearing to consider a plea bargain or sentence bargain. If the judge decides to accept a guilty plea, he may proceed immediately to sentencing. Therefore, it is essential that the judge have immediate access to the Victim Impact Statements.

Most states have a Victim Impact form which can be requested from the prosecutor, probation department, or victim advocate. If not, simply write in letter form an explanation of the emotional impact the killing of your loved one has had on your family, as well as the financial impact including medical expenses, funeral expenses, lost wages, and any medical or counseling expenses required by the family as a result of the trauma. Documentation of these expenses can result in the defendant being ordered to reimburse you. If your state statute allows, you may also include your opinion about what kind of sentence the defendant should be given.

In preparing statements, be sure your information is accurate. Write from the heart about your pain, but try not to make bitter or disparaging remarks about the offender. Judgement of the defendant belongs to the judge or jury.

### Going to Trial

If the defendant persists in pleading not guilty, the case will be set for trial. He has a constitutional right to choose whether he wants his case to be decided by a judge (bench trial) or a jury. In most jurisdictions, the State must accept the form requested by the defendant. Be prepared for numerous postponements even after a trial date has been set.

If the defendant chooses a jury trial, jury selection may take days or weeks before the trial actually begins. Most surviving families want to attend the trial although they know it will be an emotionally draining experience. Because trials can take several weeks, victim families may have difficulty getting off work to attend. Several states have now realized that victims should have the right to attend the trials concerning their loved ones without penalty, much the same as employees who are called to serve jury duty. Inquire about such statutes from your victim advocate or prosecutor. If no statute exists in your state, explain to your employer why it is important for you to be at the trial.

You may be surprised to learn that the defense may try to prevent you from attending the trial. The defense attorney's goal is to minimize the victim sympathy factor during the trial. The defense wants any sympathy to be focused on his client, the defendant, and not the victim.

A common tactic of the defense is to subpoena you as a potential witness and then ask the judge to invoke the "gag rule"—a rule stating that witnesses cannot listen to each other testify. Even though you may not be called to testify, you will, thereby, be kept out of the courtroom, never to be seen by the judge or jury. If you did not witness the crime and, therefore, would not testify until sentencing, ask the prosecutor to advocate that you be allowed in the courtroom.

*Stephanie never let me down. I had to be there to be sure the court didn't let her down.*

Roberta Roper, whose daughter,a college senior, was murdered.

*I had to go. It was my responsibility to Andy and Pam. It would be evidence of their having been alive and loved.*

Louise Gilbert, whose son and daughter-in-law were murdered.

*I don't want to be at the trial, but I can't not be there. I don't want revenge, but I do want justice. And I think that he should get the maximum if he's found guilty.*

Tinka Bloedow, whose fourteen year old daughter was killed by a drunk driver.

*We wanted to be there because no one was there to defend our daughter. The only picture the jury saw of Catina was the morgue picture. They had no idea what kind of girl she was. That's why it is so important that families be there, because the victim is not there to answer.*

Michael Salarno, whose 18 year old daughter, Catina, was murdered.

Several states now statutorily allow victims (or victim's representatives/family) to be present during the trial if they are not going to testify, or if they are, to remain in the courtroom following their testimony. One state even allows the victim to sit with the prosecutor at counsel table, just as the defendant sits beside the defense attorney.

Some prosecutors worry that the victim family may become emotionally upset during the trial and unduly prejudice the jury providing grounds for a mistrial. Assure the prosecutor that you will respect appropriate courtroom demeanor if you desire to be present in the courtroom.

Be aware of these general courthouse guidelines:

- Do not discuss the case in the halls or restrooms. Your behavior out of the courtroom is as important as your behavior in it.

- Never speak to the judge or a juror, even if you encounter them in the hall or at lunch. They must remain bias-free as they hear the evidence.

- Prepare yourself for the emotional impact of hearing the defendant say "not guilty." Even though you know you would not be in a trial unless he was pleading "not guilty," many victims report jarring emotional response when they actually hear the words. In many cases, these are the first words the family has heard the defendant speak.

- Expect to hear upsetting testimony. You may hear gruesome details for the first time. You may see photos you have never been shown before. You may also hear the defense attorney attempt to show that your loved one was responsible for his or her own death. He has an ethical responsibility to do all he can to represent his client's legal interests. Therefore, much of what is so important to you may seem like gamesmanship for players who try to out skill each other in courtroom drama. It is up to the judge or jury to determine the truth.

- If you feel you may lose control of your emotions during the trial, leave the courtroom. Your demeanor in the courtroom must not be intended to influence the judge or jury.

- If you have questions or concerns during the trial, write them down and give them to the prosecutor or victim advocate. Don't whisper during the trial.

- Victim advocates from the prosecutor's office or from support groups such as Mothers Against Drunk Driving, Parents of Murdered Children, or Compassionate Friends are usually available at your request to attend court with you and answer questions at appropriate breaks.

*The courtroom was a battlefield with combat played out between lawyers and a judge with a calm defendant dressed in his best.*

Louise Gilbert

*It was a nightmare, an absolute nightmare. When you learn of the death, you go into shock. At the trial, reality sets in. But I still feel strongly that the family needs to be there.*

Harriet Salarno, whose 18-year-old daughter was murdered.

*Finally, after a number of postponements, we sat in the small courtroom. I met the prosecutor and moments later came face to face with the man charged with killing my children. During the trial, I learned the meaning of horror, and their last hours were never again to leave my mind. Pam's fractured head and almost nude body were described in detail as well as the maggots and flies that covered her. I bolted the courtroom when the pathologist began to describe my son's bloated body.*

Louise Gilbert, whose son and daughter-in-law were murdered.

## Courtroom Procedure

Standard courtroom procedure during a criminal trial is as follows:

- Opening statements are given by both attorneys.
- The State will call witnesses to the stand in an attempt to prove that the defendant is guilty as charged. The prosecutor's questioning of each State witness is called "direct examination." The witness is then "cross-examined" by the defense attorney. The procedural rules for cross-examination are more liberal than rules for direct-examination. For example, in cross-examination, leading questions may be asked such as "Isn't it true that....?" After cross-examination, the witness is given "re-direct examination" by the prosecutor and

"re-cross examination" by the defense. The witness is then dismissed, unless either attorney plans to call the witness back in to testify later. Once dismissed, witnesses may usually remain in the courtroom. However, it is prudent to sit near the back of the courtroom out of the direct view of the judge or jury.

- After the State has presented all its witnesses, the defense will present its witnesses, going through the same procedures of direct and cross-examinations.

- After all the evidence has been presented, each side may introduce witnesses to rebut testimony previously given. Sometimes they are former witnesses not previously dismissed. Sometimes they are new witnesses.

- Each side presents closing arguments. The state has the burden of proof in the case and therefore has the right to argue both before and after the defense. Typically, the prosecutor will summarize the evidence before the defense argues and then rebut the defense's arguments.

- The judge gives the jury instructions for their deliberations, or if it is a bench trial, retires to deliberate himself.

**The Verdict**

Hearing the announcement of the verdict is the climax of the trial and usually a very emotionally laden time for the victim family. You must be aware that a legal verdict and the truth are, unfortunately, not always the same thing. While a defendant may not, in truth, be innocent, he may be proven "not guilty." Judges and juries are the best way our society knows to determine legal justice. Judges and juries are also susceptible to human error. All of this must be kept in perspective.

The standard of proof in criminal cases is "beyond a reasonable doubt," the highest burden of proof required in any trial proceeding. This term is legally undefined. However, if any doubt based on reason exists as to any element of the offense as charged, the verdict of the judge or jury must be "not guilty." Evidence must establish the facts so clearly, positively, and

138

explicitly that there can be no reasonable doubt that the case was proven.

## Sentencing Trial or Hearing

If the defendant is convicted in the adjudication phase (innocence/guilt phase) of the criminal trial, the case will proceed to sentencing. Sentencing may occur immediately following the conviction or be scheduled for a later hearing. Even though you did not witness the crime, you may be allowed to testify during the sentencing hearing.

Written Victim Impact Statements must be submitted to the prosecutor and probation departments before sentencing. They will pass them on to the judge for consideration in sentencing. If oral Impact Statements are allowed in your jurisdiction, you may be called to the witness stand to testify about the impact of the crime on your life.

*The prosecutor put me on the stand. He wanted the jury to hear first-hand about the devastating effect the killing of Stephanie had on our family. Defense objected. After a brief conference, the Judge agreed that legally, Stephanie's character and our grief were irrelevant.*

*I burned with anger. I had been silenced. Yet, the defendant's former teacher and his prison minister would both speak on the defendant's behalf. The court deemed **their** statements relevant.*

Roberta Roper, whose daughter was murdered and who later introduced legislation, now law in Maryland, that Victim Impact Statements must be heard. The right has now been upheld by the U.S. Supreme Court.

Evidence and procedures are different during sentencing, sometimes called the dispositional phase of the trial, than during the innocence/guilt phase. Defense witnesses will be giving subjective testimony about the defendant and why they feel he should receive a particular sentence.

Since the goal of your Victim Impact Statement is to convey the effect your loved one's killing has had on you, it is not expected that you testify free of emotion. Be aware, however, that judges and juries can tell the difference between genuine and contrived emotion.

You need not fear testifying if you have discussed your testimony honestly with the prosecutor and have thought through how you want to present it.

Following are some suggestions which should help you testify with relative ease and maximum credibility.

- Dress conservatively—in a business suit if you are a man, in a dress or business suit if you are a woman. Your clothing should not be flashy or in any way detract from what you are saying.

- Take notes or a written statement with you to the witness stand if you think you may need them. However, be aware that the judge, attorneys, and jury may be allowed to examine them.

- If the defense attorney asks if you have discussed your testimony with your attorney it is appropriate to respond "yes." Your attorney may have helped you organize your statement, but you are testifying to the true impact of the killing on you and your family.

- If you don't understand a question by one of the attorneys, simply say so and ask that it be repeated. If you do not know the answer to a question, say so. If you feel an attorney is trying to manipulate you into an answer that is not true, turn to the judge and tell him that you will need to explain your answer.

- Be descriptive as you speak of the impact of the killing. Describe particular events that were/are painful for you. Your goal is to enable the judge or jury to come as close as possible to understanding how you felt when it happened and how you feel now.

- Do not use jargon or judgmental words if you say anything about the offender. Words such as "drunk," "alcoholic" and "crazy" are judgmental words you should not use. Talk about your pain and avoid bitter or disparaging remarks about the defendant.

- Avoid unnecessary phrases or cliches such as "I honestly believe that...." or " I can truthfully say that...." They are less powerful than short, simple statements.

- Maintain eye contact with the attorney who has asked you the question. Don't look to your own attorney for help when being questioned by the defense attorney. Look at the judge or jury if the attorney asks you to explain something to them.

- If you request that the defendant pay restitution to your family, be prepared to present actual bills and statements of the amounts paid or owed.

- Always be honest. Take your time. Pauses before your answers indicate that you are taking the question seriously and thinking before you speak. If you approach the task of testifying with integrity, your testimony will be respected.

## Appeals

Following a conviction and sentencing, the defendant has a right to appeal the case to a higher court to consider errors in procedure or application of the law at the trial court level. You need to be prepared for this, especially if the sentence is maximal. Many convicted felons are released on appeal bonds until the appeal is heard, which may be several years later. Under the concept of "innocent until proven guilty," a trial court decision is not considered final until appeals are heard. While this hardly appears fair from the victim perspective, it is a procedural

Criminal Justice System

safeguard that has proven useful, especially if a convicted defendant was indeed innocent.

**Parole**

Sentences assessed are seldom sentences served. Primarily, because of prison over-crowding, the concept of "good time," credit given for days of imprisonment because of good behavior, is common. The convicted criminal may actually receive two or three more days credit for each day served, and in fact serve only a fraction of the actual sentence imposed.

*Judge Haile gave Jones a life sentence for murder, a life sentence for rape, and twenty years for kidnapping. But, surprising even the defense, he announced that the sentences could be served concurrently. This meant that Jones would be eligible for parole in less than twelve years with credit for time already served and credit for good behavior.*

Roberta Roper, whose daughter was murdered.

*The boy who killed our daughter was a juvenile (17). He was found guilty of criminal negligence involving a death, drunken driving, and hit and run. He was sentenced to 90 days in a chemical dependency treatment and behavior modification program, his license suspended for six months, and he was placed on probation until his nineteenth birthday.*

*I later learned that he was again charged with drunk driving when he was twenty-one. The previous conviction had not been reported to the Public Safety Department and the new charge was being treated as a first time misdemeanor. When I finally got them to look into it, I learned that within six months of his license being reinstated, he had two speeding violations and another for driving with an open bottle. We got his license suspended*

142

*again, but when the suspension was over, he was cited for an illegal turn and use of a motor vehicle in commission of a felony. Following yet another license revocation, he was cited with refusing a breathalyzer test following a drunk driving arrest. I'm enraged, absolutely enraged. I thought the system worked, but I'm not so sure now.*

Tinka Bloedow, whose daughter was killed by a drunk driver.

As soon as the convicted offender is placed in jail or prison, call there to obtain his Identification Number. Include this and his full name in all correspondence with parole boards as well as your own name and address so you can receive a response.

Send a copy of your original victim impact statement to the Parole Board. Write the parole commissioners responsible for the particular facility to which the prisoner is assigned as well as the State Parole Board. Inform the Parole Board in writing from time to time about the ongoing impact of the death of your loved one. Especially send new letters when it is time for parole review. Petitions submitted requesting continuing incarceration are often impactful at review time. Call prior to the review and ask if you may provide an oral statement. In any event, leave your phone number and ask to be informed when the review decision is made.

## Cases Against Juveniles

In most states, juvenile hearings are not open to the public including the victim's family. Juvenile case files are closed.

## Other Resources

## Writing Letters

Letter writing should be a part of all your interactions with the criminal justice system. If you feel the slightest inkling that a conversation will be forgotten or misconstrued, write a follow-up letter. It can prevent a prosecutor, probation, or parole officer from saying "I don't remember you saying..." or "I was never informed."

The League of Women Voters suggests that as you think about your letter, you consider the magic sentence, "_____ wants you to _____ because _____." Consolidating your concerns into this format will help you keep your letters clear and persuasive. Use short sentences and short paragraphs. Use action verbs such as "urge" rather than "wish". Be polite and respectful.

**Never write a letter to the judge until the offender has been found guilty. Victim Impact Statements go to the prosecutor and probation department, who will present them to the judge at the appropriate time for the sentencing hearing or trial.**

## The Media

If the killing of your loved one was sensational, or if the criminal case is unique, the media may be eager to present it in written or broadcast form. It is your right to choose whether to speak with the media. If you decide to do so, it is best to contact your attorney first. You don't want to jeopardize your case in any way. Sometimes, excessive publicity can result in a change of location for the trial.

If you speak with the media, be absolutely certain that you have your facts straight and that you refer to the defendant as the "accused" or "alleged criminal" until conviction. If you speak to a print media reporter, ask him to call and read the article to you before it goes to print, so that necessary corrections can be made.

But remember, it is acceptable to turn down an interview with the media, or refer reporters who have questions to the attorney who is handling your case. Avoiding media questions until after the trial is often the best policy.

**Ethical Review Procedures**

While the caliber of attorneys in a typical prosecutor's office is high, review procedures are available in most jurisdictions to investigate the conduct of individuals that you feel have been unethical in the treatment of your case.

Most states have a Prosecutor's Council or similarly named investigative group to look into complaints about prosecutors. Local and state bar associations also have procedures for investigating complaints and taking appropriate actions. Attorneys may be disbarred or reprimanded by the State Supreme Court in many states.

Most states have Judicial Conduct Commissions to investigate judicial misconduct.

The State Attorney General's office is usually willing to investigate professional misconduct on the part of employees of the State.

If you use these avenues to complain, be sure that you have your facts straight in filing a complaint.

**Conclusion**

Becoming an active player in the criminal justice system can add stress to your grief. You may decide that you aren't up to it and choose to let justice take its own course without your involvement. On the other hand, working in it may be an essential component in your emotional pilgrimage to get better.

Some say that regardless of the outcome, participating in the criminal justice system gave them a sense of completeness or closure. It will not cause you to grieve any less or erase the horror of your loved one's killing. But it may give you some sense of accomplishment.

The final disposition of the case can provide a historical perspective that will enable you to focus less on the offender and more on yourself and your journey toward feeling better about life.

# NOTES

# XII

---
# FINANCIAL ISSUES
---

*Those first few days after my daughter's murder, I re-
member feeling that people only wanted our money.
Everywhere we went, we were asked for cash and nobody
seemed to care why we were there.*

> Wanda Lawendel Bincer,
> whose daughter and son-
> in-law were murdered.

The financial outlay required when a loved one has been killed
can be a secondary victimization in itself. It is unfair that you
should have to pay both emotionally and financially for someone
else's malicious or negligent act.

Funeral expenses, final medical bills, travel and phone expenses, and lost wages may leave you feeling powerless and
enraged. If the person killed was a primary source of family
income, immediate financial assistance may be critical.

In order to complete the filing of various claims for financial
recovery following a death, request at least twelve copies of
certified death certificates. If your spouse was killed, copies of

the marriage license or certificate, military discharge papers, social security numbers of all family members, and birth certificates of minor children will be needed to collect benefits.

## Social Security/Veterans Benefits

These benefits are available to survivors to replace, in part, family earnings lost because of the death of a wage earner.

A surviving dependent spouse and/or children will probably be eligible. A small death benefit to assist with funeral expenses is also available to a surviving spouse or eligible minor children. Social Security and, for veterans, the Veteran's Administration, should be informed of the death immediately. It may be possible to file a claim by phone, but going in person is usually more effective. The nearest Social Security office will be in the phone book. The Veterans' Administration may be notified at Washington, D.C., 20420, or the nearest local V.A. office.

If the person killed was already drawing Social Security or Veterans Assistance and a check written to him or her arrives after the death, you must return it. If it is made out to the deceased and the surviving spouse jointly, the spouse may take it to the nearest office and it will be stamped so it can be cashed.

## Banks

All banks in which someone killed held accounts should be notified of the death. No one will have access to such accounts until an administrator is appointed. If spouses held a joint account, the surviving spouse will have access up to a certain amount. The name on the account will now have to be changed. If a joint account holds a large sum of money, a waiver may be signed to get access to the money.

A safe deposit box in the name of the deceased or jointly with someone else's name, is sealed at the time of death. Requests for access to insurance policies, etc. must be signed and witnessed.

## Life and Medical Insurance Policies

The money from a life insurance death benefit, payable to a specific beneficiary, should be immediately and automatically available to the beneficiary. However, delays are not unusual, especially if suicide is being considered as the cause of death.

All policies should be read carefully prior to filing claims. Some life insurance policies include double or triple indemnity benefits if the insured died catastrophically. Many policies include an "incontestability clause" which states that the insurance company cannot dispute the validity of a policy after it has been in force for a specified period of time.

Check everywhere that records of the deceased may have been stored to be sure all policies are located. Contact the family attorney, stockbroker, financial planner, banker, accountant, and employer. Millions of insurance dollars go uncollected every year because no one knew about the policies. In addition to policies related to employment, some unions and professional organizations offer group life and/or health insurance to their members. Carefully examine health and hospital policies to be sure you know how to file claim for payment of final medical expenses.

After all policies of the deceased have been located and examined, notify each insurance company of the death and request appropriate forms. Then check any other existing policies in which the deceased was named as a beneficiary, to change the beneficiary name. The names on automobile insurance policies will also need to be changed.

## Employer Benefits

Sometimes surviving family members do not know about employer policies because the policies are not stored in the home. Question the personnel department of the employer of the victim about all benefits, sick leave, vacation time accrued, and when checks may be expected. If dependents are covered on the health insurance policy, see how long coverage will continue. If coverage does not continue after a certain date, ask about options for a continuation policy for dependents. Often one has only 30 or 90 days to convert into a new policy, so timing is important.

If the surviving spouse is employed, his or her own policies should be checked. The deceased may also have been covered by them. After all claims relative to a death are filed, a new beneficiary will have to be named. Check all health policies to see if mental health counseling is covered in the event it is needed.

Get clarification from your own employer about whether or not vacation time will have to be taken to visit attorneys, to attend court hearings, and the multitude of other matters which must be handled during working hours. Ask if a subpoena will be required in order for you not to be penalized for attending court.

## Creditor Intervention

The unanticipated death of a family member nearly always means that ongoing bills will be set aside while immediate expenses are paid. Contacting creditors about the family crisis can be very difficult.

If the person killed was an income producer for the family, check all loan contracts, mortgages, and credit card contracts to see if there is a clause which pays the balance in the event of death. If there is, notify the creditor immediately and request claim forms.

Next, list all creditors, their addresses, and the amount owed. Then consider the amount remaining after paying immediate expenses. Determine when and how much insurance money as well as ongoing income is expected. (Be cautious about accepting inadequate insurance settlements out of fear of facing creditors.)

From these figures, determine how much, if anything, can be paid on bills in the near future. Write each creditor, explain what has happened, advise regarding how much can now be paid per month, and when payment can be expected. State that you wish to agree to a new payment schedule which will fit both your needs and the creditor's, and that if you do not hear otherwise, you will assume that the creditor agrees with the plan you have submitted.

In cases of joint accounts, inform creditors that the name on the account is now to be changed to your name. However, a surviving spouse should not assume credit cards in the name of the deceased spouse only. Credit card companies are persistent in requesting widows and widowers to sign their spouses debts over.

In some cases, emergency funds are available for bills. Public utilities such as the electric, gas or water company may extend credit if an application is completed.

In the event that a landlord is uncooperative, phone City Hall and ask for a copy of the City's Landlord/Tenant regulations. Most legal aid services also have summaries of these regulations.

It is to the creditor's advantage to work out payment schedules so he is eventually reimbursed. It is also against the law in most states for a creditor to harass or intimidate a debtor. If the creditor refuses to accept the payment plan, write another letter and send a copy to your attorney. If that fails, ask a legal aid service or attorney, hired on an hourly rate basis, to intervene.

If a trusted friend or relative is willing, ask him or her to handle all bills as they come in for a while. These bills can seem like another wave of victimization. Decide when you are ready to resume responsibility for your financial affairs.

### Automobile Insurance Benefits

Insurance practices differ from state to state. If residing in a no-fault state, costs are covered by the policy of each individual involved in the crash. This holds true even if the driver was driving someone else's vehicle. Check your state insurance code or call your State Insurance Commission at the State Capitol for defined coverage time and dollar limits. In addition to death benefits, property benefits, and medical benefits, inquire about

Financial Issues

use of a rental car, wage loss, replacement costs of services such as child care and housekeeping, and mental health counseling benefits.

In a non no-fault state, if the driver of an automobile was liable for the crash and has liability insurance, you probably will receive benefits from the liability insurance company. Eligibility conditions vary based on the insurance law in each state.

If the driver liable for the crash had no liability insurance at the time of the crash, you may be eligible to receive benefits from the uninsured/underinsured motorist provisions of your own policy. Again, the insurance laws of each state will define that eligibility.

Insurance adjustors may approach you soon after the crash. Decisions made at that time may have far-reaching financial ramifications. Be cautious.

- If you have chosen to retain a civil attorney, refer all insurance representatives to your attorney. This includes the adjustor of your own insurance company.

- If you choose to handle the claim on your own, be sure you know the company of the adjustor with whom you are speaking. If an adjustor comes to your home, ask to see a business card. If the adjustor's language is confusing, say so. Even though you may discuss the case, it is wise not to give signed or recorded statements.

- Be fully competent and aware when you discuss the case with an insurance adjustor. Grieving can make you feel numb and confused. It can cause you to have poor memory. If you are not able to discuss the case rationally with the adjustor, ask him or her to return at another time. It is a good idea to have a trusted person with you when you discuss these matters.

- In a separate insurance file, keep copies of crash reports, estimates on repairing or replacing the automobile, medical and funeral bills, and copies of any letters having to do with the insurance settlement.

- Get several estimates on damages to the vehicle before settling on property damage. These may be obtained from body shops or automobile dealers. You can negotiate the insurer's offer if you have several estimates.

- Obtain copies of **all** medical bills before settling on the medical or bodily injury damages. If others in your family survived the crash it is very important to know the full extent of injury and prognosis for treatment before making a final settlement. This may take months. Keep a daily record of adverse effects of the crash, including psychological ones. Be sure that when doctors write medical assessments, they understand the injured victim's job description, employment history, and education.

- As you discuss the insurance settlement, the company may alter their offers. Request a copy of each settlement offer in writing to avoid confusion or in the event you receive conflicting information. This does not need to be a formal typewritten letter, but may be handwritten, signed, and dated by the person making the offer.

- The adjustor may or may not be able to advise you of your claim rights based on statutory insurance law, since adjustors do not have legal degrees. You may ask to have a written copy of claim rights in your state. Be sure you know the statute of limitations for personal injury and property damage actions in your state. You may want to consult an attorney on an hourly fee basis for this information.

If you feel you are not being treated appropriately by a claims adjustor, contact his or her supervisor. If that is not satisfactory, write a personal and confidential letter to the president of the insurance company explaining what has happened. Your State Insurance Commission or State Board of Insurance may also be contacted. All legitimate insurance companies are regulated by a State Insurance Commission. Contact the switchboard at your State Capitol for the phone number. All phone or personal communication relative to a complaint should be followed up by letter.

In many states, insurance companies are required by statute to act in "good faith." In such states, this means that if claims are unreasonably denied, if valid claims are not promptly paid, or if victim families are coerced into settling for less than is due them, this behavior gives rise to a course of action against the insurance company. Punitive damages may also be recoverable upon proof of actual malice, fraud, or oppression, usually referred to as "outrageous conduct."

## Homeowner's or Renter's Insurance

Your homeowner's or renter's insurance policy will probably cover loss of contents of the car from luggage and purses including their contents to damaged clothing worn, subject to a deductible. Contact your insurer to learn how to apply. Usually an itemized list of lost or damaged items, age, and approximate purchase price is required.

## Civil Suits

If the person responsible for the death of your loved one has substantial income or assets which are recoverable, or if the liability insurance company has failed to offer a fair settlement for a claim, consider filing a wrongful death civil suit.

Civil actions are totally separate from the criminal case. While the State provides a prosecutor to try the criminal case, an attorney for a civil proceeding must be retained. Do not expect either attorney to advise on the other suit, although they should be interested in each other's case to enhance their own. Civil actions depend largely on the way in which the death occurred and the financial expenses incurred. Recovery of medical, funeral and property expenses are usually the first to come to mind. Financial recovery may be possible for more remote damages such as past and future wage loss, and past and future pain and suffering. In some states, if one spouse is killed, the other spouse can sue for loss of consortium (change in relationship). Some states also allow for punitive damages, additional money to punish the offender.

If a public entity such as the city, county or state government was responsible in any way for the death through commission or negligence, financial recovery may be possible from them as well. Traditionally, governments have been immune from civil suits. Referred to as "sovereign immunity challenges," appellate courts in a number of jurisdictions have now found them responsible for such things as inappropriate parole release, inadequate probation supervision, and failure to arrest a drunk driver who later kills someone.

In drunk driving cases, "dram shop" statutes and case law allow for the drinking establishment who negligently encouraged an intoxicated person to continue drinking, or served a person under the age of twenty-one, to be sued if that person later harms or kills someone.

To pursue any of these sources of financial recovery, you will need to hire a civil attorney. Take the following points into consideration:

- Shop around. A good recommendation from another victim is often an invaluable piece of information. Interview more than one attorney before making a decision. As you interview, ask what kind of cases they handle, how they charge, and what they think about your case. Tell them you will make the decision to retain at a later date. Remember, however, that the degree of success the attorney has in pursuing a full and fair outcome often depends on investigating the case as soon as possible after the crime was committed.

- Look for an attorney who concentrates a significant percentage of his practice on personal injury and wrongful death cases. If you use another type of attorney, note when you look at the contract whether additional fees will be required if co-counsel is retained.

- Ask if the attorney has more experience representing plaintiffs or defendants. Ask what percentage of his trials he has won. Ask what percentage of the cases settle out of court. This will help you analyze how much trial experience the attorney has, which is important.

- Ask for an explanation, in terms you can understand, of the laws in your state which relate to your case, including the statute of limitations. Ask for a brief written summary of the merits of the case as the attorney sees it at that point. This will prevent confusion later on. Be skeptical, however, of an attorney who promises certain results. Airtight cases simply don't exist.

- Be sure you understand the fee schedule. Does the attorney require a retainer fee for investigating the case? Does he work on a contingency basis (paid a percentage of the actual recovery)? Does he do any work at an hourly rate? Does he require a promissory note as security for fees? If handling your case on a contingency basis, does the percentage differ if settled out of court, if going to trial, or if going to appeal? Will you be billed for out-of-pocket expenses (court fees, deposition fees) as they occur or will they accumulate until a settlement is reached? If the case is lost, are costs or fees still owed?

- Negotiating on fees, carried forth in honest good faith, is professionally acceptable and legal in most states. If percentages are regulated by state law, the attorney should explain the statute to you.

- If negotiable, you may want to discuss an hourly fee for work on recovery for actual damages and a contingency percentage which decreases as the amount of recovery for punitive damages increases. If there is no significant dispute on liability or damages, and only the insurance is recoverable, a contingency fee may be more than fair for hours involved. The attorney may therefore work for your insurance recovery on an hourly basis.

- Be sure the employment contract to retain the attorney includes the fee schedule, is complete, specific, and clearly understood before you sign it.

- Ask the attorney for copies of all correspondence relating to your case, and request that he instruct the defendant and/or his insurance company to make all offers for settlement in writing.

- Request that bills for services be itemized and match them with the fee agreement.

- Ask for receipts indicating payment and purpose of payment each time you pay your attorney.

If you have exercised care in choosing your attorney, you will probably be satisfied with his services. Negligence in civil cases is exceedingly complex and open to a variety of interpretations. This short discussion can in no way provide information sufficient to understand the intricacies of your particular case. Only your attorney can do that. Sometimes it is impossible for attorneys to give clear and concise opinions about their cases.

If you become dissatisfied, you should discuss your concerns with the attorney. If a satisfactory relationship cannot be achieved, the attorney may be discharged. At the point of discharge, the attorney will be entitled to a fee for services rendered in keeping with the terms of the employment contract.

If you suspect that your attorney's conduct is unethical, you may file a complaint with the local bar association. State Supreme Courts may also disbar, suspend, or censure an attorney for unprofessional conduct. If you wish to take legal action against your attorney, be certain of your facts.

## Bankruptcy

Bankruptcy Law is complex and civil attorneys sometimes tell their clients prematurely that there is no value in filing a civil suit against an offender because even if he is found liable he will file bankruptcy to avoid payment. That may or may not be true.

Bankruptcy law is federal and changes have taken place during recent years to assure that criminals, including drunk drivers, cannot file personal bankruptcy under chapter 7 and 13 of the Bankruptcy Code to avoid civil judgments or to escape paying criminal restitution.

Bars and restaurants sued for irresponsibility serving those already intoxicated or those under the age of 21 may still file for corporate bankruptcy under Chapter 11.

If your civil attorney suggests that the offender may file bankruptcy, ask him to consult with a qualified bankruptcy attorney. The American Bar Association and most State Bar associations have bankruptcy sections which can refer you to qualified attorneys.

## Crime Victim Compensation

All states except Maine have Crime Victim Compensation programs which reimburse crime victim families for out of pocket, non-property expenses. These benefits were designed for victims in situations where insurance and civil recovery are not possible. Benefits include funeral expenses, medical expenses, loss of wages, and other financial needs deemed reasonable. In some states, dependents are eligible for lump sum benefits. All states with Victim Compensation programs provide for mental health counseling for injured victims and some pay for counseling for survivors of someone killed. Many states provide emergency funds which are available within a few weeks of the date of the crime.

Since regulations vary from state to state, it is wise to call the prosecutor, the police department, or a local victim group such as MADD or Parents of Murdered Children to request a Victim Compensation application. If you are still unable to learn about the program, call the switchboard of your State Capitol and ask to be connected to the person in charge of the Crime Victim Compensation Program in your state.

The crime must be reported to the police within three to five days, and the victim family must cooperate with law enforcement officials in the prosecution of the case.

If you are having difficulty with funeral expenses, inform your funeral director that you will be applying for Victim Compensation to cover the funeral expenses. He may then be willing to forego billing for the funeral for the time being.

You will be expected to submit bills or receipts with the application. Except for emergency awards, applications take weeks or months to process, so application procedures should be started as soon as possible. Additional bills may be submitted later.

## Restitution

Restitution is money or services ordered by the criminal court to be paid by the offender directly to the victim or surviving family after final conviction. The purpose of restitution is to make the offender personally accountable for his crime and to restore, in part, the victim's loss.

Victim requests for restitution can cover medical and funeral expenses, lost wages, ongoing counseling fees for survivors, or other expenses considered reasonable by the court. Requests for restitution must be accompanied by bills or receipts and should be presented to the criminal court judge through the prosecutor or probation department **prior to sentencing of the offender.** Restitution requests are usually attached to the presentence investigation prepared by the probation department.

While restitution is a very sound concept, it is not a quick or easy solution to financial stress. It is dependant upon conviction of the offender, which rarely occurs until months or years after the crime was committed. Offenders sometimes have limited income from which to pay restitution, especially if they are sent to prison. Procedures for the collection of restitution from the offender and transferring it to the victim are rarely adequate. And, once the offender is out of the criminal justice system, a means for monitoring the payments no longer exists.

Most states now require that restitution be ordered unless the judge states in the record the reasons for not doing so. A few states automatically attach a civil lien to the criminal judgement in order to assure payment after the criminal case is closed.

In most cases, unless a substantial lump sum restitution is ordered immediately following trial (which will only happen if the offender has the means to pay it), chances of actually receiving restitution are slim.

## State and County Social Services

Families with limited income and resources who are faced with the death of a loved one, may be eligible for emergency short term assistance from county social service agencies. This assistance may include vouchers for rent, utilities, food, and medication but rarely cash.

A parent of dependent children, if the wage-earner was killed, may qualify for Aid to Families with Dependent Children (AFDC) and should apply at the local State Department of Human Services or equivalent agency. Food stamps are also available for low income, low resource families. It usually takes several weeks to obtain AFDC or food stamps.

Local charities and churches willing to help may be identified through a call to United Way or local crisis hotlines. Victim witness programs and victim support groups may also be aware of financial resources.

## A Final...But Very Important...Reminder:

Try to refrain from making any unnecessary major financial decisions until a year or more after your loved one's death. Decisions about revision of your will, moving, investments, sale of properties, etc., can be considered after your life has settled down a bit and after your capacity for clear and rational thinking has been restored.

# XIII

## CONCLUSION

$\mathbf{F}$ive to ten percent of our population lose a family member to death every year. Too many of those deaths are the result of unanticipated violence.

One of the wonders of most human beings is their basic, inherent tendency toward recovery following trauma. And yet recovery is never complete after a loved one has been senselessly killed. Sorrow, anger, and frustration with injustice following such a death causes pain that is treatable, but difficult to cure. Time is a significant component. Grief work cannot be "pushed through." It is to be experienced little by little over time.

As family and friends of the deceased strive to refocus their sight on life rather than on death, they often take a step forward, fall one or two steps backward, work on it some more, and make progress. Grief spasms may continue for a lifetime. Many are astounded at the eruption of grieving when they least expect it.

It is hoped that this book will help victims and survivors feel free to express their feelings, to choose how and when they will work on feeling better, and to discard, without guilt, the ill advice of those who care but do not understand.

It is hoped that the suggestions offered will help survivors to realize that getting better means talking about what has happened. It means finding safe, supportive persons with whom to share the pain. It means being patient with themselves when progress is slow. It means finding positive things to do. It also means believing that some thread of good can come from the ashes of despair.

Successful caregiving to families enduring a sudden death, whether from loving family members, friends, volunteer victim advocates, or professional counselors, requires a gentle spirit and a great deal of patience.

It is hoped that readers undertaking the task of caregiving have learned to be more effective. Helping means being a good listener. It means refraining from being judgmental. It means avoiding cliches which attempt to talk victims out of their feelings of despair. It means reaching out in tangible ways, especially on holidays and anniversaries. It means talking fondly of memories of the deceased loved one. It means assertively guiding victims through the criminal justice process and advocating financially for them, if necessary.

Most significantly, however, it is hoped that those individuals who have been forced into pain they didn't ask for, will feel less alone and better understood than they did before. Walking in the shoes of a fellow struggler has a healing power all its own. Knowing that someone else understands something of their journey and genuinely cares is a gift to be treasured.

# RESOURCES

# Resources

# RESOURCES - ORGANIZATIONS

## National Victim Advocacy Organizations

Each of the following have current updates on victim's rights legislation and provide information and referral services to assist victims in locating their nearest local program.

American Association of Suicidology
2459 So. Ash
Denver, CO 80222
303-692-0985

Mothers Against Drunk Driving (MADD)
511 E. John Carpenter Fwy. #700
Irving, TX 75062
214-744-6233
Victim Hotline 1-800-GET-MADD

National Institute for Mental Health
5600 Fishers Lane
Rockville, MD 20857
301-496-4000

NOVA (National Organization for Victim Assistance)
717 D Street N.W.
Washington, D.C. 20004
202-393-NOVA

National Sheriff's Association Victim Program
1450 Duke Street
Alexandria, VA 22314
703-836-7837 / 1-800-424-7827

National Victim's Resource Center
P. O. Box 6000 AIQ
Rockville, MD 20850
1-800-627-NVRC(6872) / 301-251-5525

Office for Victims of Crime
633 Indiana Avenue, N.W.
Room 1352
Washingtyon, D.C. 20531
202-724-5947

Samaritans (Suicide)
500 Commonwealth Ave.
Boston, MA 02215
617-247-0220 (24 hours)
617-247-8050 (Teens)

National Victim Center
307 W. 7th Street
Suite 1001
Fort Worth, TX 76102
817-877-3355

Victims of Crime Resource Center
McGeorge School of Law,
University of the Pacific
3200 Fifth Ave.
Sacramento, CA 95817
1-800-Vic-tims (Calif.) / 916-739-7049

American Bar Association
Victim/Witness Program
c/o Susan Hillenbrand
1800 M Street NW
Washington, D.C. 20036
202-331-2260

## National Headquarters of Support Organizations

Parents of Murdered Children
100 E. 8th Street, B-41
Cincinnati, OH 45202
513-721-LOVE

Compassionate Friends
P. O. Box 3696
Oakbrook, IL 60522-3696
708-990-0010

Concerns of Police Survivors (COPS)
9423 A Marlborouth Pike
Upper Marlborough, Maryland 20772
301-599-0445

## National Resources re: Civil Suits

American Trial Lawyers Association
1050 31st Street N.W.
Washington, D.C. 20007
202-965-3500

Crime Victims Litigation Project
c/o National Victim Center
4530 Ocean Front
Virginia Beach, VA 23451
804-422-2692

Trial Lawyers for Public Justice, P.C.
1625 Massachusetts Ave. S. 100
Washington, D.C. 20036
202-797-8600

## National Insurance Organizations

National Association of Independent Insurers
2600 River Road
Des Plaines, IL 60018
312-297-7800

Alliance of American Insurers
1501 Woodfield Road, Suite 400 West
Schaumberg, IL 60173-4980
312-330-8514

## National Medical Resources

American Trauma Society
1400 Mercantile Lane
Suite 188
Landover, MD 20785
1-800-556-7890

National Head Injury Foundation
333 Turnpike Rd.
Southborough, MA 01772
617-879-7473 / 1-800-444-NHIF

Sunny Von Bulow Coma & Head Trauma Foundation
555 Masison Ave. #32001
New York, NY 10022
212-753-5003

Spinal Cord Society
Rt. 5, Box 22A, Wendell Rd.
Fergus Falls, MN 56537
218-739-5252

American College of Emergency Physicians
P. O. Box 61991
Dallas, TX 75261-9911
214-550-0911

**National Funeral/Burial Resources**

Conference of Funeral Service
Examining Boards
15 NE 3rd St.
P. O. Box 497
Washington, IN 47501
812-254-7887

National Funeral Directors Association
11121 W. Oklahoma Ave.
Milwaukee, WI 53227
414-541-2500,
(FISCAP - arbitrates consumer
complaints)

# READING RESOURCES FOR ADULTS

Augsburger, David. *Caring Enough to Forgive/Not to Forgive,* Regal Books, 2300 Knoll Drive, Ventura, CA 93003.

Austern, David. *The Crime Victim's Handbook,* Penguin Books, 40 West 23rd St., New York, NY 10010.

Bard, Morton, and Sangrey, Dawn. *The Crime Victim's book,* Brunner/Mazel, Psychological Stress Series, 19 Union Square, New York, NY 10003.

Bolton, Iris. *My Son My Son,* Bolton Press, Atlanta, Georgia.

Carlson, Lisa. *Caring for Your Own Dead,* Upper Access Publishers, One Upper Access Road, P. O. Box 457, Hinesburg, VT. 05461.

Cato, Sid. *Healing Life's Great Hurts,* Chicago Review Press, 213 W. Institute Place, Chicago, IL 60610.

Donnelly, Katherine F. *Recovering From the Loss of a Child,* Macmillan Publishing Co., 866 3rd Ave., New York, NY 10022.

Donnelly, Katherine F. *Recovering From the Loss of a Sibling.* Dodd, Mead & Company, 71 Fifth Avenue, New York, NY 10003.

Gaylin, Willard. *The Killing of Bonnie Garland,* Penguin Books, 40 West 23rd St., New York, NY 10010.

Gray, Martin. *For Those Loved,* Little, Brown and Company, 34 Beacon St., Boston, MA 02108.

Grollman, Earl A. *Living When a Loved One has Died,* Beacon Press/Fitzhenry & Whiteside Ltd., Toronto, Canada.

Grollman, Earl A. *What Helped Me When My Loved One Died.* Beacon Press, 25 Beacon Street, Boston, Massachusetts 02108.

Grollman, Earl A. *Talking About Death: A Dialogue Between Parent and Child,* Beacon Press, 25 Beacon Street, Boston, Massachusetts, 02108.

Hewett, John. *After Suicide,* Westminster Press, Philadelphia, PA.

Knapp, Ronald J. *Beyond Endurance:When a Child Dies,* Schocken Books, 62 Cooper square, New York, NY 10003.

Kubler-Ross, Elisabeth. *On Children and Death,* Macmillan Publishing Company, 866 Third Avenue, New York, NY 10022.

Kushner, H.S. *When Bad Things Happen to Good People,* Avon Books, 1790 Broadway, New York, NY 10019.

LaTour, Kathy. *For Those Who Live,* P.O. Box 141182, Dallas, Texas 75214, (for surviving siblings).

Lord, Janice Harris. *Beyond Sympathy,* Pathfinder Publishing, 458 Dorothy Ave., Ventura, CA 93003.

Manning, Doug. *What to Do When You Lose a Loved One,* Harper & Row, 151 Union St., San Francisco, CA 94111-1299.

Neiderbach, Dr. Shelly. *Invisible wounds:* Crime Victims Speak, Haworth Press, 28 E. 22nd Street, New York, NY 10010.

Osterweis, Marian et al Eds. *Bereavement: Reactions, Consequences and Care,* National Academy Press, 2101 Constitution Avenue NW, Washington, D.C. 20418.

Rando, Therese A. *Parental Loss of a Child,* Research Press, 2612 N. Mattis, Champaign, IL 61821.

Rando, Therese A. *Grieving: How to Go on Living When Someone You Love Dies,* Lexington Books, 125 Spring St., Lexington, MA 02173.

Ross, Betsy E. *After Suicide: A Unique Grief Process*, Betsy Ross, Iowa City, Iowa.

Saldona, Theresa. *Beyond Survivial, Bantam Books, 666 Fifth Ave., New York, NY 10103.*

Schaefer, Dan and Lyond Christine. *How Do We Tell the Children?* Newmarket Press, 3 E. 48th Street, New York, NY 10017.

Schiff, Harriet S. *The Bereaved Parent,* Penguin Books, 40 W. 23rd Street, New York, NY 10010.

Schiff, Harriett S. *Living Through Mourning,* Viking-Penguin, 40 W. 23rd St., New York, NY 10010.

Westberg, Granger E. *Good Grief*, Fortress Press, Philadelphia, PA.

Staudacher, Carol. *Beyond Greif: A Guide for Recovering from the Death of a Loved One,* New Harbinger Publications, 2200 Adeline St., Suite 305, Oakland, CA 94607.

Stearns, Ann K. *Living Through Personal Crisis,* Thomas More Press, 223 W. Erie Street, Chicago, IL 61610.

Stone, Howard. *Suicide and Grief,* Fortress Press, Philadelphia, PA.

Tengbom, Mildred. *Help for Bereaved Parents,* Concordia Publishing House, 3558 S. Jefferson Ave., St. Louis, MO 63118.

*When Hello Means Goodbye* (when infants die before, during or shortly after birth) Perinatal Loss, 2116 NE 18th Avenue, Portland, OR 97212.

Wolterstorff, Nicholas. *Lament For a Son,* William B. Eerdmans Publishing Company, 255 Jefferson Avenue SE, Grand Rapids, Michigan 49503.

## READING RESOURCES FOR CHILDREN

Blume, Judy. (for teens), Dell Books.

Bunting, Eve. A Sudden Silence, (older children) Harcourt Brace Jovanovich Publishers, 1250 Sixth Ave., San Diego, CA 92101.

Buscaglia, Leo. *The Fall of Freddie the Leaf*, (elementary age) Holt, Rinehart, Wilson.

Clardy, Andrea F. *Dusty Was My Friend*, (elementary age), Human Sciences Press, 72 Fifth Ave., New York, NY 10011.

Cunningham, Julia. *Wings of the Morning*, (elementary age) Golden Age Books.

Green, Phyllis. *A New Mother for Martha*, (elementary age), Human Sciences Press, 72 Fifth Avenue, New York, NY 10011.

Heegaard, Marge. *When Someone Very Special Dies*, (small children), Woodland Press, 99 Woodland Circle, Minneapolis, MN 55424.

Johnson, Joy & Marv. *Tell Me, Papa*, Centering Corporation, Box 3367, Omaha, Nebraska 68103-0367.

Krementz, Jill. *How It Feels When a Parent Dies*, (older children) Alfred A. Knoph. 201 E. 50th St., New York, NY 10022.

Linn, Erin. *Children Are Not Paper Dolls*, The Publishers Mark, P.O. Box 6939, Incline Village, NV 89450.

Mellonie, Bryan and Ingpen, Robert. *Lifetimes*, (small children), Bantam Books, 666 Fifth Avenue, New York, NY 10103.

Powell, E. Sandy. *Geranium Morning*, (elementary age) Carol-Rhoda Books, Minneapolis, Minnesota.

# INDEX

# ORDER FORM

Pathfinder Publishing of California
458 Dorothy Ave.
Ventura, CA 93003-1723

Telephone (805) 642-9278   FAX (805) 650-3656
Book Order Telephone Line: (800) 977-2282

Please send me the following books from Pathfinder Publishing:

_____Copies of **Beyond Sympathy** @ $11.95                          $____
_____Copies of **Injury** @ $9.95                                    $____
_____Copies of **In Search of My Husband's Mind** @$22.00            $____
_____Copies of **Living Creatively**
                 **With Chronic Illness** @ $11.95                   $____
_____Copies of **Managing Your Health Care** @ $9.95                 $____
_____Copies of **No Time For Goodbyes** @ $11.95                     $____
_____Copies of **Quest For Respect** @ $9.95                         $____
_____Copies of **Sexual Challenges** @ $11.95                        $____
_____Copies of **Surviving an Auto Accident** @ $9.95                $____
_____Copies of **Violence in our Schools, Hospitals and**
                 **Public Places**   @ $22.95 Hard Cover             $____
_____                                @ $14.95 Soft Cover             $____
_____Copies of **Violence in the Workplace** @ $22.95 Hard           $____
                 **Violence in the Workplace** @ $14.95 Soft         $____
_____Copies of **When There Are No Words** @ $9.95                   $____
                                               Sub-Total             $____
                 Californians: Please add 7.25% tax.                 $____
                 Shipping*                                           $____
                                               Grand Total           $____

I understand that I may return the book for a full refund if not satisfied.
Name:_____

Address:_____
_____   ZIP:_____

*SHIPPING CHARGES U.S.
Books: Enclose $3.25 for the first book and .50c for each additional
book. UPS: Truck; $4.50 for first item, .50c for each additional. UPS
2nd Day Air: $10.75 for first item, $1.00 for each additional item.
**Master and Visa Credit Cards orders are acceptable.**